NEW LABOUR,
NEW LANGUAGE?

Norman Fairclough

Routledge
Taylor & Francis Group

LONDON AND NEW YORK

First published 2000
by Routledge
11 New Fetter Lane, London EC4P 4EE

Simultaneously published in the USA and Canada
by Routledge
29 West 35th Street, New York, NY 10001

Reprinted 2001, 2003

Routledge is an imprint of the Taylor & Francis Group

© 2000 Norman Fairclough

Typeset in Bembo by Taylor & Francis Books Ltd
Printed and bound in Great Britain by Biddles Ltd, Guildford and
King's Lynn

British Library Cataloguing in Publication Data
A catalogue record for this book is available from the British Library

Library of Congress Cataloging in Publication Data
Fairclough, Norman, 1941–
New labour, new language? / Norman Fairclough.
Includes bibliographical references and index.
1. Great Britain—Politics and government–1997– 2. Political
oratory–Great Britain–History–20th century. 3. English
language–Political aspects–Great Britain. 4. Socialism–Great
Britain–History–20th century. 5. Politicians–Great Britain–Language.
6. Blair, Tony, 1953–Language. 7. Labour Party (Great Britain) I. Title.
DA592.F34 2000
808.5´1´088351–dc21   99–046501

ISBN 0–415–21826–8 (hbk)
ISBN 0–415–21827–6 (pbk)

EW LABOUR NEW LANGUAGE?

To those of us who find ourselves carried along helplessly in
Tony Blair's rhetorical stream of consciousness, Norman
Fairclough offers a life-saving branch to which we can cling,
while we work out where we are and where we are being
swept.

(Simon Hoggart)

It's time to 'bin the spin!' Is New Labour's 'new politics for a new
Britain' just rhetoric, just empty words?

This is a book about the politics of New Labour that focuses on
language. Norman Fairclough gets behind the rhetoric to uncover
the real meaning. He examines a wide range of political speeches and
texts, from Tony Blair's speech following the death of Diana to the
1997 Labour Party Manifesto and Bill Clinton's book *Between Hope
and History*.

New Labour, New Language? blows open the whole debate on the
nature of the political discourse of New Labour and the 'Third Way'.
Written in a clear, non-technical style and including a glossary, *New
Labour, New Language?* will appeal to anyone interested in language or
politics.

Norman Fairclough is Professor of Language in Social Life at
Lancaster University and the author of many books, including
Language and Power (1989).

CONTENTS

PREFACE

Bin the spin!

Is New Labour's 'new politics' for a 'new Britain' just rhetoric, just empty words? Does the Government's notorious taste for 'media spin' mean that presentation becomes more important than policy, rhetoric more important than substance? This is a book about the politics of New Labour which focuses on language. It's a critique of the language of New Labour.

Why focus on language? Because language is crucial in the politics of New Labour. Language has always been important in politics, but the way New Labour does politics makes it more so. Why for instance did the Labour Party change its name to 'New Labour'? According to one of its key advisers, Blair 'knew that only by contrasting "new" Labour with "old" Labour explicitly would the electorate believe that Labour had changed and could be trusted'.[1] In other words, changing the name wasn't just reflecting a shift in political ideology, it was manipulating language to control public perception.

The public relations industry (to which Gould belongs) is at the heart of New Labour, which calculatively manipulates language. The phenomenon is not new, but the scale and intensity certainly are. Despite a rhetorical commitment to decentralising government, New Labour firmly manages the political and governmental process from the centre (Blair is widely perceived as a 'control freak'). Part of this is governing by 'media spin', constantly monitoring and manipulating how issues are presented in the media. This is largely a matter of making sure the right language is used – for instance, making sure that the approved expression 'public–private partnership' is used rather than the dreaded 'Tory' term 'privatisation'; and avoiding the even more dreaded 's'-word 'socialism'). Managerial government is partly managing language, and this also includes managing the language of the leader, Tony Blair – not only the content of what he says, but the values which are conveyed through his style of saying things: decency, common sense, 'middle England', compassion, toughness, and so forth. For instance, Blair is very good at showing care and compassion in the way he talks and in his 'body language', and New Labour's impression managers have built upon this gift. New Labour understands that it is not enough to talk about 'values' (which it often does), it also needs a language that conveys the values for which it claims to stand.

What about policy? New Labour is committed to a 'Third Way', which they claim transcends the 'old' division between left and right. There is an immediate question about rhetoric and substance: the 'Third way' is much talked about, but it is by no means clear that it is a distinctive political position. Some would say it is Thatcherism with a few frills.

New Labour is totally committed to the neo-liberal global economy, and actively supports international initiatives to enhance the tendency towards 'globalisation', e.g. extending free trade. There are winners and losers in globalisation. It is the winners who are eager to extend it, and New Labour basically backs the winners (despite its claim to 'tackle' the 'social exclusion' of the losers). One important resource in extending globalisation is controlling the language in which it is represented. For instance, in the political language of New Labour, 'globalisation' and 'the new global economy' are represented as accomplished facts rather than partial and uneven tendencies, and 'change' is represented as an inevitable movement in the direction of globalisation. The language of New Labour tells us 'there is no alternative' – neo-liberalism is something with which we have to live. It also represents its commitment to international neo-liberal policies, such as the reduction of welfare spending, in ways that rhetorically dress up what is going on – for instance by using what Stuart Hall has called the 'weasel word' – 'reform'.[2]

The language of the 'Third Way' is a rhetoric of reconciliation – 'economic dynamism as well as social justice', 'enterprise as well as fairness'. The 'old' politics misguidedly thought you had to choose between these, but you don't! The language of New Labour is full of such expressions with the sense of 'not only this but also that'. But saying that we can have both this and that, both 'economic dynamism' and 'social justice', tells us nothing about the relationship between them. Do energies and resources go equally to achieving 'economic dynamism' and 'social justice'? Don't we need to limit 'economic dynamism' if we want 'social justice'? How can we do this except through using the power of the state to control the economy? Doesn't New Labour's absolute rejection of state 'interference' in the economy mean that the language of the 'Third Way' is just that – mere words, empty rhetoric?

ACKNOWLEDGEMENTS

My thanks to The Random House Group Ltd for granting permission to reproduce extracts from: Bill Clinton (1996) *Between Hope and History*, Hutchinson, and to the following for their help and/or encouragement in the preparation of this book: Zsazsa Barát, Lilie Chouliaraki, Romy Clark, Mick Dillon, Simon Hoggart, Costas Iordanidis, Anna Jordanidou, John O'Neill, Andrew Sayer, Elena Semino, Roland Wales. And thanks to Zsazsa for helping me refocus when I temporarily lost track. My thanks to Nick Smith of the Linguistics Department of Lancaster University for his work on compiling the corpora of New Labour and earlier Labour texts.

Norman Fairclough

NEW LABOUR, NEW LANGUAGE?

An introduction

At the end of 1998, the British 'New Labour' Government had something of a crisis: two Cabinet ministers resigned in the face of accusations of financial impropriety. The worst blow was the loss of Peter Mandelson, the Minister for Trade and Industry, one of the chief architects of New Labour and of its electoral victory, and one of the closest allies of the Prime Minister, Tony Blair. Mandelson's departure led to intense speculation over a shift in direction on the part of the Government; in one formulation at the time: a move towards rather less of the 'new' and more of the 'Labour'. The Deputy Prime Minister John Prescott was widely interpreted as advocating such a shift. This was the interpretation which was for instance put on an interview he gave to the *Independent*,[1] in which he said 'we need to get away from rhetoric and back on to the substance of government'. That statement apparently constituted the basis for the *Independent's* headline: 'Prescott bins the spin for real policies'. 'The spin' is an allusion to New Labour's 'spin-doctors', the people responsible for the media presentation of the Government and for putting a media 'spin' (or angle) on its policies and activities. Media communications are more carefully handled and more centrally controlled by the New Labour Government than any previous British government, and the Government has been accused by its critics of governing by media spin. Mandelson himself had overall responsibility for media communications as the Minister without Portfolio before he was shifted to the Department of Trade and Industry. He was closely associated with New Labour's reputation for being preoccupied with spin, and credited with being the spin-doctor par excellence.

John Prescott was interviewed on the BBC Radio 4 'Today' programme a few days after the interview in the *Independent*.[2] He was at pains on that occasion to deny that there were any major divisions over policy or strategy within the Government. Indeed he returned to the contrast between 'rhetoric' and 'substance', but used it to set the Government against the press – given the manifesto undertakings it has implemented, the Government 'is a government of substance, of traditional values in a modern setting', it is the press that 'are not really interested in that substance', that go in for 'rhetoric'. But 'rhetoric' seems quite an appropriate way of describing what Prescott is doing here: having taken the opportunity of Mandelson's resignation (as well as Blair's absence abroad on holiday) to publicly air divisions within the Government and to take a position, he neatly relocates the 'rhetoric versus substance' issue as a criticism not of the Government but of the press. If politicians are to successfully pursue internal divisions in public in contemporary mediatised politics, they need the sort of skills Prescott is manifesting in this case: being able to venture a criticism in a sufficiently ambivalent way that one can draw back from it if challenged without bringing into question the unity of the Government or Party or one's own loyalty.

This is how the interviewer, Jim Naughtie, responded to Prescott:

> You've made your point very clearly. The point though is that the way that people in government talk about these things is important, you'd acknowledge that. Indeed it was Mr Mandelson's credo that the way you talked about things, they way you used language was very important, because it sent out messages. And you don't need to be told that a lot of Labour MPs – when they saw what you were saying, the language you were using, 'traditional values' albeit 'in a modern setting' – were saying: 'Look, here at last is a little more of the stuff we want to hear. He doesn't talk about "The Project" doesn't talk about "New Labour", he talks about "Labour".'

And Prescott's answer was:

> Yes but then that is presented as a kind of great division. It's not a division because I'm pointing out to you the things that every one of us support …. the traditional values in a modern setting, what I'm saying is perhaps we should emphasize it a great deal more.

Naughtie is combining, perhaps confusing, two issues. One is the issue of what 'messages' politicians convey to one another through shifts of language – one way of seeing politics is as an ongoing struggle to achieve dominance of one political position over others which is partly enacted as a struggle for the dominance of political language, a struggle for instance to win acceptance for formulations like 'traditional values in a modern setting' rather than the 'Third Way', or 'Labour' rather than 'New Labour'. Naughtie is suggesting that this is what Prescott was doing in the interview, but Prescott rejects the implication of a division within New Labour: the question is only how much 'emphasis' is given to parts of what he implies is a shared language. Again, Prescott seems to be rhetorically covering over internal differences.

The second issue is the perception very much associated with Peter Mandelson that the language which politicians use 'sends messages' to the public, from which it has been seen to follow that the language has to be tightly monitored to make sure that it sends the 'right' message, or in favoured New Labour parlance is 'on message'. In fact one question that Naughtie asks Prescott is whether on this occasion he abided by Government policy that all ministerial media statements should be 'checked' by the Prime Minister's press office (headed by another formidable spin-doctor, Alistair Campbell). Prescott's rather sour reply was that he had 'talked to people' about what he 'was going to say' – he seems to avoid using the word 'check', which would imply the Deputy Prime Minister (Prescott) being subject to the judgement of an unelected official.

Language, politics, and government

Language has always been important in politics and in government (I don't see politics and government as the same thing – I shall draw a distinction between them below). Political differences have always been constituted as differences in language, political struggles have always been partly struggles over the dominant language, and both the theory and practice of political rhetoric go back to ancient times. Language has therefore always been a relevant consideration in polit-ical analysis. But language has become significantly more important over the past few decades because of social changes which have trans-formed politics and government. An important part of these changes is a new relationship between politics, government and mass media – a new synthesis which means that many significant political events are now in fact media events (for instance, a TV interview with the Prime Minister can itself be a major political event). There has been what one might call a 'mediatisation' of politics and government. The particular genius of Peter Mandelson has perhaps been in seeing that these changes may have more radical implications for the nature of politics and government than has so far been realised. Mandelson has not been alone in seeing this: to a degree what he has done is bring to British politics developments which have been going on elsewhere, particularly in the USA. But there is also a process of change which is being referred to in the USA, Britain and internationally as the 'reinvention of government',[3] which entails a greater focusing of language. I shall discuss this below.

One consequence of the 'mediatisation' of politics and government is the transformation of political leaders into media personalities. This probably started in Britain with Harold Macmillan in the 1950s. Tony Blair's immensely successful populist leadership style is comparable in certain respects with Margaret Thatcher's, though very different in other respects. The communicative style of leaders is now recognised as a crucial factor in political success or failure, and Labour is acutely aware of this because their recent history has included failures, notably Michael Foot but also to some extent Neil Kinnock. Communicative style is a matter of language in the broadest sense – certainly verbal language (words), but also all other aspects of the complex bodily performance that constitutes political style (gestures, facial expressions, how people hold themselves and move, dress and hairstyle, and so forth). A successful leader's communicative style is not simply what makes him or her attractive to voters in a general way, it conveys certain values which can powerfully enhance the political 'message' (see further below).

New Labour claims to be a 'new politics'. According to Tony Blair, 'ideas need labels if they are to become popular and widely understood. The "Third Way" is to my mind the best label for the new politics which the progressive centre-left is forging in Britain and beyond'.[4] Notice two things about this: first, the 'Third Way' is being 'forged'; second, 'forging' it is linked to making it 'popular and widely understood'. The 'Third Way' does not come ready-formed, nor is it forged once-and-for-all. On the contrary, New Labour politicians are constantly forming and formulating it, in speeches, newspaper articles, books and pamphlets, official documents, etc. They are constantly working on making coherent connections between the policies and ideas – 'enterprise', 'flexibility', 'welfare-to-work', 'social exclusion/inclusion', 'participation', 'fairness', and so forth. The 'Third Way' is constantly being talked into being, new language is constantly being found to bring these elements together into a coherent whole. This is a process that cannot be completed – circumstances keep changing, and differences within New Labour are worked through in different formulations, differences of language. And crucially this is going on in public – there is no clear line between finding policies that work and finding policies that win consent. As Franklin puts it, 'New Labour' is perhaps the first government genuinely committed to the view that presentation is part of the process of policy formation'.[5] Analysing the shifting language of the 'Third Way' is an essential part of getting to grips with the 'new politics' of New Labour.

At the same time, New Labour is involved in a 'reinvention of government' which in itself entails a greater salience for language. In part, this is a matter of a new form of control from the centre based upon business corporation models, including promotional means for managing consent. This involves 'government by media spin', but also what Blair has referred to as 'experiments in democracy' through for instance 'focus groups' and 'citizens' juries', which allow the Government to develop its policy in a way that incorporates public opinion from the start. But the centralised management of political communication in the New Labour Government seems to be at odds with another aspect of the 'reinvention of government' – the Government's commitment to 'devolving power and making government more open and responsive'.[6] This includes a certain dispersal of government, which is indicated by the concept of 'participation' – a great many task forces, reviews and advisory groups have been set up with memberships that bring together the Government, business, voluntary organisations and other sections of society. Many groups and people who have hitherto not been involved in government are being drawn in, and it is in that sense that government is becoming more dispersed.[7] However, this does not mean that the centre has given up control – it is a dispersal, but not a fragmentation. In so far as 'partnership' becomes a reality rather than just a rhetoric (see below), it entails a new form of control that crucially involves language – shaping the culture, discourse and language of the dispersed agents of government rather than directly controlling what they do.

This book is about the language and rhetoric of New Labour. It is not just a book about language for people who are interested in language. It is also a book about politics and government for people who are interested in politics and government. It is a book about politics and government that approaches them through language, as language; or, to use a term that has come into fashion recently, as 'discourse'. I think it is appropriate to write a book about New

Labour which centres upon language for the reasons I have begun to indicate above – to sum them up, because (as New Labour politicians are aware) language is becoming an increasingly prominent element of the practices of politics and government. This does not mean that it was not important before – its inherent importance has become clearer as its prominence has increased. I think the main point of writing such a book is that a focus on the language of New Labour can enhance our understanding, as well as analysis, of the politics of New Labour.

New Labour is widely seen as a major break in British politics and government, and as such it has aroused a great deal of controversy (to which I have already begun to allude). A focus on language can contribute to debate on controversial issues. Let me sum up three:

- What is the 'Third Way'? Is it really any more than a veiled form of Thatcherism or neo-liberalism?
- How does New Labour's promise of more open government square with the centralised and tightly managed way in which it actually governs?
- Tony Blair has developed a very successful style, but is there any political substance beneath it?

Analysing political language

We can identify three different aspects of political language which I have referred to in the discussion above: the communicative style of political leaders, the political discourse associated with a particular party or group (in the case of New Labour, the political discourse of the 'Third Way'), and the way language is used in the process of governing (or 'governance'). These are the three main concerns in this book, so I shall say a little more about each of them now.

Blair's rhetorical style

Tony Blair's style has been immensely successful. Perhaps the clearest example before the NATO war against Yugoslavia (discussed in chapter 4 and chapter 6) was his widely acclaimed success in 'capturing the popular mood' after Princess Diana's death in the autumn of 1997.[8] Here is the beginning of the short statement he made on that occasion:

I feel like everyone else in the country today – utterly devastated. Our thoughts and prayers are with Princess Diana's family – in particular her two sons, two boys – our hearts go out to them. We are today a nation, in Britain, in a state of shock, in mourning, in grief that is so deeply painful for us.

Why were these words so effective in 'striking a chord' with many people?[9] One important point is that it was not just his words but his overall bodily performance, the way he looked and acted, as well as what he said. But the language was an important factor. Notice in particular that it is a mixed language. There are two threads running through it. Let me 'extract' one of them:

Our thoughts and prayers are with Princess Diana's family, in particular her two sons, our hearts go out to them. We are today a nation in mourning.

This is the conventional sort of language that leaders use to speak on behalf of the nation on such occasions. Blair uses the first person plural ('we'), and predictable, pre-constructed expressions (clichés) – 'thoughts and prayers', 'our hearts go out to them', 'a nation in mourning' (once you hear 'our hearts' for instance on this sort of occasion, you can predict 'go out'). But threaded into this conventional public language is a more personal language (Blair begins speaking for himself, in the first person singular, and about his own feelings) and a more vernacular language. It is as if Blair (with his advisers – the speech has been attributed to Alistair Campbell) had started with the official form of words, then personalised and informalised it. He uses a vernacular language of affect as well as a public one – 'utterly devastated', 'in a state of shock'. Notice also the way he rewords 'her two sons' as 'two boys', which again is a shift between a more formal way of referring to them in terms of their relationship to Diana and a more intimate, family way. Blair says he feels 'like everyone else' – he is not only speaking formally for 'the nation', he is also speaking informally for ordinary people; and part of the power of his style is his ability to combine formality and informality, ceremony and feeling, publicness and privateness.

A crucial part of the success and apparent continuing popularity of Blair's style is his capacity to, as it were, 'anchor' the public politician in the 'normal person' – the necessary posturing and evasions of politics are it seems at least partially redeemed by Blair's capacity to reassert constantly his normal, decent, likeable personality. In his speeches and interviews there is always a mix between the vernacular language of the normal person and the public language of politics. The sort of 'normal person' that comes across is very much 'middle-class' and 'middle-England' in values, outlook and style. Blair's communicative style embodies the 'new politics' of the 'Third Way' in this respect, as also in the way he has learnt how to be 'tough' and how to assert moral authority in the way he speaks.

But Blair's leadership personality and style are not pre-given, they are carefully constructed. For instance, according to Gould,[10] New Labour learnt the political advantage it could gain from being 'tough' and talking about being 'tough' (including using the word so often) from research on focus groups – Blair's 'toughness' has been self-consciously built into his communicative style as a matter of policy and strategy. Blair's apparent and claimed preference for acting on the basis of his political 'instincts' is at odds with the careful calculation of effects on 'public opinion' which goes into every move that he and New Labour make.[11] Blair is, according to his biographer Rentoul, an accomplished showman, an actor. Of course, the circumstances of contemporary politics are not of his making – all politicians have to act, to pretend, or to put it more harshly (though not unfairly) to 'live a lie'. But individual leaders can respond to those circumstances in various ways – by trying to be more accomplished at pretending than others, or by doing what they can to change the circumstances. Perhaps the charitable view of Blair is that it is not yet clear which he will do, but the fear must be that his is a particularly accomplished show. Certainly, there is some evidence that the claims, which his communicative style implicitly makes, about the way he relates to others are at odds with the way he actually relates to them – stories about Blair as a 'power freak' in the managing of the Government (including the Cabinet), the parliamentary Labour Party, and the Labour Party overall, are at odds with the polite, cooperative, open and relaxed personality conveyed in his communicative style. In this sense, leadership styles can 'lie'.

Tony Blair may stand for New Labour in the popular imagination, but New Labour is in fact a rather disparate alliance of different political positions associated with different communicative styles (that of his deputy, John Prescott, for example). Although the emphasis in this book will be on Blair, it is important not to lose sight of these differences. Another important issue to keep in focus is how distinctive New Labour is, both from its predecessors in Britain and from similar political positions in other countries. This is relevant to questions of rhetorical style, as well as to the other two aspects of the language of New Labour I shall be dealing with – what similarities, for instance, are there between Margaret Thatcher and Tony Blair, or Bill Clinton and Tony Blair? Is the Blair rhetorical style a purely local and individual achievement, or is it part of a wider cultural change? See chapter 4 for further discussion.

The political discourse of the 'Third Way'

The 'Third Way' is (as I said above) ongoingly constituted and reconstituted as a discourse in the documents, speeches, interviews, etc. of New Labour. We can see it as a continuing process of representing the social world from the particular position New Labour occupies in the political 'field' – others in other parties, and in other tendencies within the Labour Party, represent it differently (and there is even variation within New Labour). It is an ongoing representation of the world as it is now, of the world as it might be and should be according to New Labour, and of government itself as a process of acting to change the world. From this perspective the 'Third Way' is a creation in language, something that is constructed in discourse. An important part of grasping and analysing the 'Third Way' is therefore analysing how it is constructed in discourse.

I have already referred to the continuing attempts by New Labour politicians to reformulate the 'Third Way' as a coherent and compelling idea. One aspect of such formulations is marking out the relationship and difference between the 'Third Way' and the political positions it is represented as displacing and transcending – in one formulation, the 'old-style intervention of the old left and the laissez-faire of the new right',[12] or, in the example below, 'the intrusive hand of state intervention' and 'the destructive excesses of the market'. The pamphlets, speeches and newspaper articles of New Labour politicians are full of descriptions of how the 'Third Way' differs from the 'old left' and 'new right', often in the form of extended lists* such as the following in which what had hitherto been seen as incompatible opposites are represented as reconciled:

THIRD WAY – OUR VALUES

There is a clear theme running through the annual report. It is the third way. There is something genuinely new about the politics of this government. When you look at the record of the past year ask yourself:

What other government this century would have cut corporation tax to help business yet introduced a minimum wage to help the poorest paid?

What other government would have given financial independence to the Bank of England as well as setting up a unit to deal with homelessness?

What other government would work so hard to offer jobs, and new skills to young people as well as cracking down on youth crime?

What other government would reform the workings of government to make the centre of government stronger and more strategic, yet devolve power dramatically to local people throughout Britain?

What other government would put huge extra resources into health and education yet still keep to tough overall spending ceilings?

This is the third way. A belief in social justice and economic dynamism, ambition and compassion, fairness and enterprise going together.

The third way is a new politics that helps people cope with a more insecure world because it rejects the destructive excesses of the market and the intrusive hand of state intervention. It is about an enabling government that gives people the chance of a better future in which all people can play their part.[13]

The phrase 'not only … but also' pervades the political discourse of New Labour in a variety of expressions (e.g. 'enterprise *yet also* fairness', 'enterprise *as well as* fairness', 'enterprise *with* fairness', 'enterprise *and* fairness' (with the *and* stressed, i.e. italicised), which both draws attention to assumed incompatibilities, and denies them. It is a rhetoric of denial of expectations – things are not as they have been thought to be.

The discourse of the 'Third Way' is a representation of New Labour politics which inevitably invites comparison between what New Labour says and what it does. The term 'rhetoric' is often used in this connection – in one of the various senses that 'rhetoric' has, it points to the possibility that words are 'empty', that they are 'mere words' which are at odds with action. The issue is a crucial one because the central controversy about New Labour is whether its 'Third Way' is indeed a new form of centre-left politics as it claims, or a somewhat disguised continuation of the neo-liberal politics of the new right. In other words, does it only transcend the division between 'old left' and new right in words, or are the words of 'Third Way' politics in harmony with action? For instance, is the claim 'rejects the destructive excesses of the market and the intrusive hand of state intervention' mere words, or are actions being taken which prevent the destructive excesses of the market without recourse to state intervention? What are these actions – indeed, what could they possibly be? Is there any way except the power of the state for preventing these excesses? (See further below.)

Of course, at this point analysis of the language of New Labour has to be combined with broader analysis of New Labour as a government – we cannot answer the question about 'rhetoric' simply by reference to language. But language is relevant – one aspect of pervasive meaning 'not only ... but also' in formulations of the 'Third Way' is that the two previously incompatible terms that are made compatible (e.g. 'social justice and economic dynamism') are constructed as equal, as having equivalent weight. There may be policies oriented to 'social justice', but they may be secondary or marginal in comparison with policies oriented to 'economic dynamism'. Moreover, the listing syntax which is also pervasive in constructions of the 'Third Way' treats pairs of terms that may be radically different as equivalent – it is easy to be carried along by the 'rhetoric' in a rather different sense of that term, the persuasive patterning of the language (in this case, the repeated questions beginning 'What other government would ...?'). Contentiously, one might say that the power of rhetoric is used to portray what some commentators[14] see as the potentially fatal contradictions of New Labour as its greatest strengths.

The language of government

I said earlier that government and politics, though of course closely connected, are not the same thing. I see politics as struggle amongst groups of people over substantive aspects of social life, including centrally struggles over the distribution of social 'goods' in the widest sense. What characterises politics from a language perspective is disagreement, dissent and polemic.[15] I see government as the management of relations between groups whether within nation-states or within organisations on a lesser scale (the term 'governance' is now widely used to cover the range). Different regimes of government are more or less open to politics – they can politicise issues or attempt to depoliticise them, the latter through a reduction and attempted marginalisation of politics.

Democratic government depends upon achieving a sufficient measure of consent for particular intended effects in social life. There are various ways in which consent can be achieved. It can be achieved politically through dialogue in which disagreement and dissent can be expressed. One of the criticisms of New Labour has been that it is intolerant of dissent, and that it takes active measures to silence dissent within the Government and the Labour Party, as well as more widely.[16] Although New Labour constantly initiates 'great debates' and calls for debate and discussion around its policy initiatives (e.g. welfare reform), it seems in broad terms that it sets out to achieve consent not through political dialogue but through managerial methods of promotion and forms of consultation of public opinion (e.g. in focus groups) which it can control. The Government tends to act like a corporation treating the public as its consumers rather than as citizens.

The New Labour way of governing (or 'governance') is in part a way of using language. One issue is the ways in which New Labour's language of government is promotional rather than dialogical. Let me take the process of reforming the welfare system as an example, and note three ways in which language works promotionally within that process, and therefore in a way that discourages dialogue and debate (for a more detailed analysis, see chapter 5). First, the overall process is carefully stage-managed. For instance, the Green Paper (the Government's consultation document) on welfare reform was published in March 1998.[17] Its publication was preceded by a series of meetings around the country addressed by the Prime Minister and a series of papers published by the Department of Social Security making the case for welfare reform. These were widely seen as preparing the ground. Each initiative was accompanied by a press release. The management of the process is partly the management of language – there is a constant process of summarising the proposed welfare reform, selecting particular representations of it, particular wordings, that will be most effective in achieving consent. In other words, media 'spin'. The process is promotional, not dialogical, although it was referred to as a 'debate'.

Second, the Green Paper itself is univocal, monological. In the real world of welfare there are many voices, many opinions on what the problems are and how they should be resolved. Yet a striking feature of the language of the Green Paper is that there is very little reported speech – very few reports about what various relevant people or groups have said or written on the issue of welfare reform. Certain central 'players' in the real world of welfare are virtually and, in some cases, totally absent from the document – the staff who 'deliver' welfare, the professional experts who work within the welfare system or write about it, various claimant or campaigning organisations.

Third, the Green Paper does not engage its readers in dialogue. Of course there are few direct readers of such official documents, but there are millions of indirect readers (so to speak), people who hear or read reports about it in the media. The document is organised with such indirect readers in mind – its first chapter is a summary of the whole document that many journalists will draw upon, and there is also a press release about the document, as well as a preface by the Prime Minister. The focus throughout is upon telling people about the Government's proposed solutions to what it takes to be the problems of the welfare system. Telling people about them is not just a matter of informing them; it is a matter of promoting these solutions, and you cannot at all easily initiate dialogue over problems you take for granted and solutions you are promoting. Again, this is evident in certain features of the language. Although there are a great many unanswered questions in undertaking such a huge policy change, there are virtually no questions in the Green Paper – readers are hardly ever asked, they are told. And although in the nature of things there is a great deal of uncertainty, readers are told things as if they were certain – there are no 'maybes' or 'perhaps'. Neither questions nor 'maybes' sit easily within promotion. The following paragraph gives some idea of the promotional flavour of the document:

> 3.7 Our comprehensive welfare to work programme aims to break the mould of the old, passive benefit system. It is centred on the five aspects of the New Deal for:
> * young unemployed people;
> * long-term unemployed people;
> * lone parents;
> * people with a disability or long-term illness; and
> * partners of the unemployed.

The Government is referred to in the first person ('our'), its programme is referred to positively (it is 'comprehensive', it aims to 'break the mould') and the existing system negatively ('old', 'passive', and a 'benefit' rather than 'welfare' system), and the common promotional device of bullet points is used – a device that may be 'reader-friendly', but is by the same token 'reader-directive', and does not encourage dialogue.

Genres, discourses, and styles

To sum up, I am suggesting that there are three analytically separable focuses in the analysis of the language of New Labour and of political language more generally: styles, discourses, and genres. Styles (e.g. Tony Blair's style) are to do with political identities and values; discourses (e.g. the discourse of the 'Third Way') are to do with political representations; and genres are to do with how language figures as a means of government (so the Green Paper constitutes a particular genre, a particular way of using language in governing). Let me stress that these are only analytically separable – in actual cases they are always simultaneously in operation. So any speech by Tony Blair for instance can be looked at in terms of how it contributes to the governing process (how it achieves consent, for instance), how it represents the social world and the political and governmental process itself, and how it projects a particular identity tied to particular values – that is, in terms of genre, discourse, and style. In other words, language is so to speak part of the action (genre), as well as representing the action (discourse), and it's also part of the performance (style).

New Labour in context

In discussing Tony Blair's rhetorical style above, I asked whether it should be seen as his individual style or part of a wider cultural change that incorporates and helps make sense of the styles of other leaders, Bill Clinton for instance (as well as Margaret Thatcher). There is a more general issue here: to what extent are the sort of changes in leadership style, politics, and governance I have been referring to a specifically New Labour phenomenon, and to what extent are they more international? Is there for instance an emergent new international centre-left politics and governance encompassing social democratic parties in other European countries as well as the Democrats in the USA? And if so, what is its relationship to neo-liberalism – is it an alternative to neo-liberalism, or conversely a position within or variant of neo-liberalism? Is, therefore, the language of New Labour part of a much more pervasive change in the language of politics and government? One objective of the book will be modestly to begin the major task of drawing international comparisons by looking at materials from the USA (the New Democrats and Bill Clinton), international organisations like OPEC and the World Bank, and the European Union.

If one danger is isolating New Labour from wider changes it may be a part of, another is overlooking internal diversity within it. I have already alluded to this in terms of the fact that New Labour is an alliance between people (like Tony Blair and John Prescott) whose positions are in some respects different, and in terms of shifts in the political discourse of New Labour in response to shifting circumstances. The diversity of positions within New Labour is linked to the nature of the wider alliance it is trying to build – in particular between the traditional 'core' of Labour supporters and the middle class. New Labour's position is a contradictory one with inherent tensions that manifest themselves in shifts and hybridities within its language. For instance, although it tends to replace 'poverty' with 'social exclusion' in representing the 'losers' in contemporary social life, 'poverty' is periodically thematicised in response to fears about losing touch with 'core supporters' (see chapter 2 and chapter 3). Moreover, the language of New Labour is inevitably an embattled language – it is contested by opponents within the Labour Party, in other political parties (Conservatives, Liberal Democrats, Greens), in trade unions, in social movements and campaigns (e.g. Friends of the Earth) – and its development is shaped through contestation with these other positions.

Criticising the language of New Labour

This book seeks to illuminate New Labour politics and government through a focus on language. I came to the book with a particular view of New Labour that has developed in the course of writing it. In common with many others, I see the politics of New Labour as rather different from how it represents itself, and as constituting a sharp break with the 'old' Labour Party. The crucial starting point for the politics of New Labour is acceptance of the new international economic liberalism – 'the new global economy' in its own terms – as an inevitable and unquestionable fact of life upon which politics and government are to be premised. My interest in the politics and language of New Labour starts from my view that it is profoundly dangerous for my fellow human beings for this new form of capitalism to develop unchecked, both because it dramatically increases inequality (and therefore injustice and suffering) and because it threatens to make life on earth ecologically unsustainable. I see my analysis of New Labour as within the tradition of critical social science – it seeks knowledge for purposes of human emancipation (rather than for instance to make organisations work more efficiently). Of course, we all have to make our own judgements about what is emancipatory (e.g. what can contribute to reducing inequality), so the important thing is that such judgements should be made explicitly and be open to question and challenge, along with the analysis.

I both describe the language of New Labour and criticise it. Part of my concern is to achieve a clearer understanding of how language is used by New Labour, but that is linked to my concern to see how language figures in the dangerous politics of New Labour – what gaps for instance arise between 'rhetoric' and 'reality' (see chapter 6). Let me briefly elaborate what I have already said about reasons for taking a language focus in analysing New Labour. New Labour is firmly committed as I have said to accepting economic neo-liberalism – a commitment that includes an attempt to change the economic policies of the European Union towards an acceptance of 'flexibility' (a word that tends to stand for the whole neo-liberal project). It is correspondingly opposed to interventions by the state to direct or control the market or to redistribute wealth created in the market – despite claims to differ from the Conservatives in claiming a role for government in providing 'opportunity', they share a common antipathy to state power. Yet New Labour claims continuity with the Labour Party's commitment to social justice and to protecting people from the negative effects of the market. This is a circle that cannot in my view be squared in reality: the state is the only real defence against the barbarism of the market. So one view of New Labour is that they seek to achieve rhetorically what they cannot achieve (given their neo-liberal commitments) in reality – a reconciliation of neo-liberal 'enterprise' with 'social justice'. Language on this account is crucial in the case of New Labour.[18]

Who the book is written for, and how it is organised

The book is written for a broad readership that is expected to include people who have a general interest in its topic, as well as people who have more specialist interests in either politics or language. It is written in a non-technical way so as to be accessible to as wide a readership as possible. Inevitably, certain specialist terms are used for analysing language, but these are kept to a minimum, and readers will find brief glosses on them in the Glossary. Items entered in the Glossary are marked with an asterisk on their first occasion of use. The book consists of six chapters in addition to this introduction. Chapters 1–3 deal with the political discourse of the 'Third Way', chapter 4 with the style of Tony Blair, and chapter 5 with the language of government under New Labour. The concluding chapter, chapter 6, discusses the relationship between 'rhetoric' and 'reality' in New Labour, with particular reference to the NATO bombing of Yugoslavia. It also discusses theoretical assumptions about language in the book, and describes my approach to discourse analysis ('critical discourse analysis'). The way in which the book is written allows readers to dip into it at various points – it does not have to be read from beginning to end, though inevitably later chapters do build to some extent upon earlier ones (that is particularly true for the first three chapters on the 'Third Way').

The book is based upon a wide range of New Labour texts (in the broadest sense). These include Labour Party documents (such as the 1997 'Election Manifesto'), books and pamphlets (e.g. Fabian pamphlets by Tony Blair and Gordon Brown, but also pamphlets by opponents of New Labour, a book by Bill Clinton, etc.), Government documents (e.g. White Papers and Green Papers on issues such as welfare reform and education), speeches by Blair and other Labour leaders as well as Margaret Thatcher, newspaper articles by New Labour leaders, and so on. These sources are listed in the References at the end of the book. I have concentrated mostly on speeches by Tony Blair not only because he dominates New Labour but also because his speeches cover the full range of New Labour political concerns and policies.

I have also compiled a computer 'corpus' of New Labour texts (as well as a smaller one of earlier Labour texts for comparison), which can be searched to give all instances of particular words or phrases.[19] The New Labour corpus includes much of the material listed under Sources, but also additional material (e.g. extra speeches of Blair's). On the basis of a comparison between the New Labour and earlier Labour material, as well as a comparison of New Labour with larger, more general corpora of contemporary English, it is possible to identify 'keywords' of New Labour, words that occur relatively most frequently.[20] The strongest New Labour keywords on the basis of this comparison are:

we	Britain
welfare	partnership
new	schools

people	crime
reform	deliver
promote	business
deal	tough
young	

I shall periodically insert into the text a summary of information from the corpus about one or more New Labour 'keywords'. I shall begin here with 'new' and related words.

Renewal, modernisation, and reform

'New' occurs 609 times in 53 speeches of Tony Blair's between 1997 and 1999 (for comparison, 'modern' occurs 89 times, 'modernise/modernisation' 87 times, and 'reform' 143 times). The most frequent collocations* are 'New Labour' (72 instances) and 'New Deal' (70 instances). The sense of political renewal conveyed by 'New Labour' is also evident in references to a 'new politics' (4 instances) and a 'new centre and centre-left' (2 instances). Political renewal is linked to national renewal in the slogan 'New Labour, New Britain', first used at the 1994 Labour Party conference. 'New Britain' is quite frequent (15 examples), and 'new' is also applied (7 times) to other international entities that Britain belongs to (e.g. 'New Europe', 'New Commonwealth'), and even the world (6 instances, e.g. the 'new world we are helping to bring into being'). Political and national renewal are linked to the 'new times' we live in – 34 instances, including also 'new era' and 'new millennium'. And there is a striking number of expressions (41 instances in all) for 'new ways of working' in government (that phrase occurs 8 times, 'new ways' 15 times, and 'new approaches' 11 times) and new relationships associated with them ('new partnership(s)' occurs 13 times). Another prominent set of meanings relates to ideas and attitudes (36 instances in all, including 'new ideas' (7 instances) 'new confidence' (4 instances), 'new sense of hope (or purpose, or urgency)' (5 instances), and there are 20 expressions referring to 'new opportunities' or 'new challenges'). Many 'new' Government initiatives are referred to (57 instances in all), such as the 'new active Community Unit', or a 'new National College for School Leadership', though unlike the 'New Deal' the adjective 'new' is not part of the title.

Despite the impression picked up by satirists that 'new' applies to everything and anything ('New Labour, new underwear'), it is used quite selectively for national, political, and governmental renewal in 'new times' which generate new opportunities and challenges and call for new approaches, ideas, and attitudes. It is perhaps 'modernise' that tends to be used more indiscriminately: 'modernisation' applies to the Labour Party, Britain, the Constitution, the Health Service, education and schools, the welfare state, defence, the Common Agricultural Policy, etc. In 25 cases 'modernisation' (or in a few cases 'modernise') is used in a general way without reference to a specific domain (e.g. 'money for modernisation' (the phrase occurs 3 times), or 'it is modernisation for a purpose' (5 instances)).

A striking contrast between 'modernisation' and 'reform' is that the former is overwhelmingly used with reference to the UK, whereas the latter is roughly equally used with reference to the EU. There is also a striking difference in terms of what is 'reformed' as opposed to 'modernised': the collocation 'economic reform' occurs 11 times, and 'reform' occurs 12 times with 'markets' ('labour', 'capital', or 'product') as its object, always with reference to the EU. By contrast, 'modernise' occurs only once with 'markets' as its object (and then the reference is to the EU) and once with 'the economy' as its object. So, economic change is 'reform' not 'modernisation', and it applies only at EU level, not in Britain. The only changes in Britain that are referred to as 'reforms' more frequently than 'modernisations' are 'welfare reform' and 'reform of the House of Lords'. Hall[21] refers to the word 'reform' in the former as a 'weasel word' which effectively masks the 'ambiguity and duplicity' of New Labour around welfare reform – is the welfare state being wound up, or truly transformed?

I shall be commenting on transcriptions from speeches and inter-views at various points in the book. It is misleading to use the punctuation conventions of written language to transcribe spoken language, because the latter is not made up of sentences beginning with capital letters and ending with full-stops. So I shall not use either of these, nor other punctuation devices such as commas or semi-colons. I shall however mark pauses to give some indication of how things were said, using a dot for a short pause and a dash for a long pause. Giving a fuller indication of what the words sound like would require marking intonation, stress, and other features – that goes beyond the scope of this book.

1

THE 'THIRD WAY'

The political discourse of New Labour

My concern in this chapter is with how the world is represented from one position in the political 'field' – that of New Labour. This includes representations of the world as it has been in the past and is now, as well as of the world as it might be and should be – a vision of the world, partly actual, partly potential. It includes representations of the economy, of work, of crime, of the family, and so forth. It also includes representations of politics and government as ways of changing the world – specifically of what is claimed to be a 'new politics', the politics of the 'Third Way'. Different positions in the political field give rise to different representations, different visions – New Labour's vision of the world is different from that of its political opponents. Looked at from a language perspective, different representations/visions of the world are different 'discourses'.

But a party has to build a coherent and distinctive representation of the world; it is not an automatic effect of position. For instance, the Conservative Party at present (early in 1999) is in some disarray not just because New Labour won a landslide victory in the 1997 general election, but more because New Labour has built a new political discourse that has incorporated elements of the political discourse of Thatcherism, and has thus transformed the field of political discourse. So the Conservatives are in difficulties which have a lot to do with questions of language. The Conservatives have the difficult task of repositioning themselves in the field, much as Labour did in the years before 1997. At present they lack a coherent and consistent political discourse, they speak in many voices rather than one. However, the consistency and unity of a political discourse is only relative: there are diverse discourses and voices within New Labour too, but there is also a sufficient commonality to give the sense of a broad unity and consistency of vision.

But this unifying political discourse is not a once-and-for-all achievement; it is constantly put at risk by events and changing circumstances, and it demands continuous work to sustain it. It is therefore constantly in flux, constantly being adapted and changed, and unevenly so across the diverse domains and activities of politics and government. These shifts are part of the shifting relations within New Labour, between New Labour and other positions in the British political field, political fields in other countries, and other fields (such as business) in Britain, the European Union, and internationally. There is also a constant movement between foreground and background — areas of the political discourse that are clearly delineated at one moment will be only roughly sketched in at another. There are areas of clarity and coherence, but also areas of vagueness and contradictions. The overall picture is a complex one.

In response to this complexity, my main account of the political discourse of New Labour in this chapter and the two following ones will be in two distinct stages. The first (in chapters 1 and 2) will emphasise the coherence of the political discourse, its inner logic. That coherence is real enough, but it is only part of the picture, and it would be misleading on its own. It will therefore be complemented by a second stage (in chapter 3), which will look at the political discourse of New Labour 'in motion' so to speak — in a way that emphasises its fluidity, variability, unevenness, and incompleteness. Chapter 1 will give an overview of the political discourse of the 'Third Way', while chapter 2 will focus on a particular aspect of this political discourse — the construction of 'social exclusion' and 'social inclusion'.

I shall proceed in this chapter by following the logic of the political discourse of the 'Third Way'. That logic begins from assumptions about the global economy that lead to an emphasis on competition between Britain and other countries, which foregrounds a project of 'national renewal' designed to improve Britain's competitive position in which there is an inclusive focus on 'one nation' and on necessary transformations of 'civic society' and of the 'deal' between government and people. A crucial assumption is that the measures necessary to strengthen enterprise in the new knowledge-based economy are also the means of achieving greater social justice. This logic is consistent with a 'new politics' which transcends the division between ('old') left and ('new') right. This vision and this logic are constituted in the language of New Labour, and my concern here is to chart how. Because my concern at this stage is with the coherence of this political discourse, I shall draw upon a limited range of sources dating from 1998 and early 1999.

The global economy

The political discourse of the 'Third Way' is built upon certain assumptions about the nature of the contemporary economy; what is referred to in Blair's speeches as 'the new global economy'. My first concern is therefore with the questions: What vision of the contemporary economy is constructed in the texts of New Labour? What goes on in the global economy according to New Labour? What are its processes? And who are represented as participants in these processes? Who are the agents that do things or make things happen? Who is affected by these processes? Here as elsewhere, language is not just a transparent medium for reflecting the way things are. On the contrary, language constructs the world (in this case the global economy) in one way or another according to position or perspective – we can evaluate different constructions in terms of their adequacy, but there is no getting away from their positioned nature.

The ghost in the machine: the multinationals

Let us begin with the following extract from the White Paper on competitiveness and the building of a 'knowledge-driven' economy:

> In the increasingly global economy of today, we cannot compete in the old way. Capital is mobile, technology can migrate quickly and goods can be made in low cost countries and shipped to developed markets. British business must compete by exploiting capabilities which its competitors cannot easily match or imitate ... knowledge, skills and creativity ...[1]

This extract from the White Paper is of some interest because it is the only point in a document that is very much focused on the global economy where there is an apparent allusion (in the second sentence) to the multinational corporations and their activities. The point is that many analysts see the multinational corporations as dominating the global economy, and that has long been the view of the left. Yet even in this extract the multinationals are not directly represented as social actors, they are not explicitly present in the text.

The second sentence is about processes* that are often represented as actions on the part of the multinationals. Yet that is not the way these processes are represented here (recall that words marked with an asterisk are included in the Glossary). Two of them (*goods can be* *made in low cost countries, (goods can be) shipped to developed markets*) are indeed represented as actions, but without any responsible agents. Grammatically, these are passive* sentences without agents. Another (*capital is mobile*) is not represented as an action at all, but as a relation of attribution, though the attribute (*mobile*) does imply action ('can be moved'), but again without a specified agent. The fourth (*technology can migrate quickly*) is perhaps the most interesting: it is represented as an action, but *technology* is represented as itself an agent in a process rather than something that is acted upon (i.e. moved) by the multinationals. Notice the metaphor* here – technology 'migrates', like birds in winter. The sentence might be differently worded, for instance as: 'The multinational corporations can quickly move capital and technology from place to place, and they can make goods in low cost countries and ship them to developed markets.' But this is not just a change in the wording; it is a change of discourse: in the discourse of New Labour, the multinational corporations are not agents responsible for what happens in the global economy. (An effect of the elision of the multinational corporations is that when 'business' figures in the political discourse of New Labour it is nearly always British business, giving an anachronistic representation of business as national, which is in contradiction with the emphatic recognition of the reality of the 'new global economy'.)

What are we to make of this? We might ask why these processes are implicit, whereas other processes in the global economy are explicit – for instance, competition between nation-states. Is this difference of conceptual or rhetorical significance – that is, is it a matter of how New Labour sees the global economy, or a matter of how they chose to represent it in public? It would be interesting to know whether these processes and their agents are equally implicit in more private internal discussions amongst New Labour politicians. Be that as it may, it is not difficult to see that foregrounding what are often represented as the destructive, self-interested activities of the multinational corporations would be problematic within the logic of the 'Third Way', which is anchored in a recognition (and indeed embracing) of the global economy in its present form as simply a fact of life that we cannot change.

One way of interpreting the extract above rhetorically is that it allows New Labour to have it both ways – to claim recognition of the activities of the multinationals without foregrounding them. Such shadowy presences of the multinationals in the margins of New Labour discourse may be politically important: New Labour is trying to hold together a rather diverse alliance, which means that it has to address (and 'keep on board') different constituencies simultaneously, including its own left wing. From this perspective there is an advantage in vagueness – in ways of representing processes that are unspecific i.e. do not specify details of processes such as who is involved and in what ways (as well as details of time, place, etc.). The more unspecific they are, the more open to various interpretations by differently positioned readerships – readers can interpret 'capital is mobile' and 'technology can migrate quickly' as alluding to the activities of the multinational corporations, or even to specific examples of capital or technology being moved by them, but they don't have to. However, even such veiled allusions to multinational corporations are rare.

Abstract actors and 'nominalisations'*

If the multinationals are not explicit agents in the global economy, there are other agents that are explicit, including agents which have an abstract character. The following is the opening of a speech by Tony Blair to the Confederation of British Industry:[2]

> I believe in this country, in its people and our capacity to renew Britain for the age in which we live.
>
> We all know this is a world of dramatic change. In technology; in trade; in media and communications; in the new global economy refashioning our industries and capital markets. In society; in family structure; in communities; in life styles.
>
> Add to this change that sweeps the world, the changes that Britain itself has seen in the 20th century – the end of Empire, the toil of two world wars, the reshaping of our business and employment with the decline of traditional industries – and it is easy to see why national renewal is so important. Talk of a modern Britain is not about disowning our past. We are proud of our history. This is simply a recognition of the challenge the modern world poses.
>
> The choice is: to let change overwhelm us, to resist it or equip ourselves to survive and prosper in it. The first leads to a fragmented society. The second is pointless and futile, trying to keep the clock from turning. The only way is surely to analyse the challenge of change and to meet it. When I talk of a third way – between the old-style intervention of the old left and the laissez-faire of the new right

– I do not mean a soggy compromise in the middle. I mean avowing there is a role for Government, for teamwork and partnership. But it must be a role for today's world. Not about picking winners, state subsidies, heavy regulation; but about education, infrastructure, promoting investment, helping small business and entrepreneurs and fairness. To make Britain more competitive, better at generating wealth, but do it on a basis that serves the needs of the whole nation – one nation. This is a policy that is unashamedly long-termist. Competing on quality can't be done by Government alone. The whole nation must put its shoulder to the wheel.

There are various processes and social actors represented here, which I discuss later, but I focus first on processes involving agents of a more abstract and impersonal character in the global economy: 'the new global economy refashioning our industries', 'change that sweeps the world', 'to let change overwhelm us, to resist it or to equip ourselves to survive and prosper in it', 'the challenge the modern world poses'. Notice the metaphorical character of these processes: 'change' is successively metaphorised as something like a tidal wave ('change that sweeps the world', 'let change overwhelm us'), implying inevitability; as a person or group to 'resist'; and as a place we can 'survive' and 'prosper' in. And the 'modern world' is personalised as someone who 'poses challenges'. The inevitability of change is also implicit in the representation of resistance as 'trying to keep the clock from turning' – 'change' is as inevitable as the passage of time.

Although change is most obviously seen as a complex set of processes, it is not represented here as a process but rather as a causal entity in other processes. It is 'nominalised', the word 'change' is used not as a verb but as a noun. Nominalisation involves abstraction from the diversity of processes going on, no specification of who or what is changing, a backgrounding of the processes of change themselves, and a foregrounding of their effect. In backgrounding the processes themselves, nominalisation also backgrounds questions of agency and causality, of who or what causes change. Yet many of the changes listed have been substantively contributed to by decisions on the part of business (including the multinational corporations referred to above) and governments to act in one way rather than another, for instance in negotiating multilateral agreements on trade and the movement of capital. The absence of responsible agents further contributes to constructing change as inevitable. And one effect of the lists of changes in the third and fourth sentences (beginning 'In technology …') is to iron out important distinctions in this regard – changes in 'family structure' are more adequately represented as changes without responsible agents than changes in 'trade'.

One effect of nominalisation is that 'change' and 'us' are constructed as two separate entities that are external to each other, one of which can affect the other. 'Change' (including the new global economy) is something that comes to 'us' from the outside, of which 'we' are not a part. This is evident in the three choices that are given for responding to change: whether it 'overwhelms' us, or we 'resist' it, or we 'survive' and 'prosper' in it. 'We' and 'it' are represented as separate and discrete entities that may come into various types of contact. 'We' are confronted with change as effects without agency, rather than being participants in change able to affect its direction.

'(The new global) economy' is also a nominalisation – though less obviously so. Instead of representing economic processes as people applying means to materials to produce things, the actual processes and people and things involved are backgrounded, and we have instead 'the economy' as an entity. The phrase 'the new global economy' presupposes★ that there is a new global economy – that is, it takes it for granted, as something we all know. The new global economy, or globalisation, is a pervasive presupposition in the discourse of New Labour. Here is another example: 'the driving force behind the ideas associated with the Third Way is globalisation because no country is immune from the massive change that globalisation brings'.[3] Globalisation is presupposed as something given and achieved. Yet most analyses of globalisation see it as an uneven and partial tendency – the economy may show globalising tendencies, but it is far from fully global (it also, for instance, shows tendencies to split into regions, like the EU). Bourdieu[4] has written about how those who aspire to a more global economy (including the most powerful sections of the existing economy, including the banks and the multinational corporations, and political parties that support them) routinely represent it as already in existence – that is they presuppose it, as New Labour does. Such presupposition can be called ideological: it is the powerful using discourse to enhance their power.

But the presupposition of a global economy can mean one of two things: either 'the fact that the economy is now global in scale', or 'the global economy in its present (i.e. neo-liberal) form'. This ambiguity is systematic in the discourse of New Labour, and it is an important one: the whole logic of the 'Third Way' flows from it.

Many of those who do see globalisation as undeniable and irreversible do not by any means see the currently dominant neo-liberal form of globalisation as inevitable and irreversible.[5] But the discourse of New Labour fudges this distinction, and in effect it constructs neo-liberalism itself as a given and irreversible fact of life. As Blair says, 'the driving force behind the ideas associated with the Third Way is globalisation', meaning globalisation in its neo-liberal form. If we challenge this, the logic of the 'Third Way' begins to unravel.

The 'cascade of change' and the logic of appearances

A favourite rhetorical device of New Labour is the 'cascade of change'[6] – lists of changes in the world that seem designed to persuade people that the changes New Labour is proposing are a part of an inevitable process. For example, from the extract above from Blair's speech to the CBI:

> We all know this is a world of dramatic change. In technology; in trade; in media and communications; in the new global economy refashioning our industries and capital markets. In society; in family structure; in communities; in life styles.

Different types of change are set up as equivalent, although the order in which the changes are listed is of no real significance, indeed what items are included in or excluded from the list matters less than their cumulative effect in signifying that the world is changing (and therefore by implication, we have to change too).

New Labour political discourse is full of such lists. They also appear for instance in representations of 'social exclusion' in terms of a combination of factors, including unemployment, poor housing, crime, and drugs – needing 'joined-up' government to 'tackle' them (see chapter 2) – and in characterisations of the 'Third Way' (see the final section of this chapter). The factors or elements in such lists are seen as connected only in the sense that they appear together. There is no attempt at explanation that tries to specify deeper relations amongst them (e.g. of cause and effect) which might constitute a system. This is a logic of appearances that manifests itself grammatically in a propensity towards lists, which is in contrast with a different logic in the left and social democratic tradition – a relational and explanatory logic that tries to make sense of appearances by looking for systems.

I discussed the multinational corporations above as a ghost in the machine. But there is a further and more abstract ghost in the machine: the system and logic of modern capitalism which positions agents including the multinationals and governments in processes such that they will act, they have to act, in certain ways. It is not just the multinationals as agents that are missing – that would suggest we can simply blame it all on them! New Labour has no analysis, still less critique, of the modern capitalist system.

Competition between nations

If the multinational corporations are not social actors in the New Labour representation of the global economy, then (apart from abstract agents like 'change' or 'the global economy') who are the social actors? In the first of the two extracts above, from the White Paper on competition, nation-states are actors in the global economy in processes of competition, with Britain as protaganist ('we'/'British business') and others (Britain's 'competitors') as antagonists. The global economy is pervasively represented in the language of New Labour as an arena of competition between nation-states. In sharp contrast with political discourse on the left, the main social actors in global economic competition are nation-states rather than multinational corporations. This is an important step in the logic of the 'Third Way': if Britain is forced into increasingly intensive competition in a global economy whose nature is unquestionable and unchangeable, then in the words of the second extract above 'making Britain more competitive' becomes the primary task for government.

The representation of Britain and other nation-states as competitors depends upon an equivalence* between Britain ('us') and British business that is implicitly set up in the texts of New Labour. In the extract above from the White Paper on competition, the first sentence includes 'we cannot compete in the old way'. An antithesis* is set up between this and the third sentence – between 'cannot compete in the old way' and 'must compete by exploiting capabilities which its competitors cannot easily match or imitate'. This contrast is the vehicle for a substitution that seems so 'natural' it easily escapes notice – 'we' in the first sentence changes to 'British business' in the third. They are implicitly set up as equivalent. It is always an implicit equivalence – we do not find explicit claims such as 'British business stands for all of us' (or 'for Britain as a whole'). But it is a perfectly routine and rather frequent equivalence that implicitly carries such a message.

There is actually a more elaborate 'chain' of equivalence, which is illustrated in the first sentence of Blair's CBI speech (in the second extract above – 'I believe in this country, in its people and our capacity to renew Britain for the age in which we live.'). This implicitly sets up the following equivalences: 'Britain' = 'country' = 'people' = 'we' ('our'). These words are simply substituted for each other, rather like pronouns* substitute for nouns. An indication of this is that we can rewrite the sentence reordering them without really changing the meaning – e.g. 'I believe in us, in the British people and their capacity to renew the country for the age in which we live.' The main point however is that the representation of the global economy as competition between nation-states rests upon the constant 'commonsensical' equivalence of country, nation, and business.

Business

There are 195 instances of 'business' in the New Labour corpus. A total of 48, i.e. a quarter of all instances, occur in collocations which relate to partnership or cooperation between business and government, and in some cases other sectors of social life such as trade unions and the voluntary sector. 'Business' collocates with 'partnership' ('with' or 'between') 19 times (e.g. 'The third way is to try to construct a partnership between government and business'), with 'involvement' 6 times, with 'links' 4 times, and then less frequently with 'cooperation', 'consultation', 'collaboration', 'work (with)', 'dialogue', 'interface', 'relations', 'relationships', 'bring together', as well as in the collocations 'bring business into government' and 'welcome business into government'. New Labour is twice referred to as 'the party of business', and another major set of collocations is clustered around helping business (26 instances in all, e.g. 'what other government would have cut corporation tax to help business'): 'help' (4 times), 'promote' (4 times), and then less frequently 'boost', 'empower', 'enhance', 'encourage', 'back', 'be positive towards', 'protect from burdens', 'contribute to developing', 'opportunities for', 'benefits to', 'improve the framework for', 'be on the side of', 'deliver stability for', 'give greater certainty to', 'offer a new deal to'. There are also 4 references to 'burdens' on business. Both the 'partnership' and 'helping' collocations are striking in terms of their over-wording* – the proliferation of different words with roughly similar meanings. A third significant set of collocations is to do with creating or expanding business (15 in all). These are the main groups of collocations for 'business' (there are also more predictable and less interesting ones such as 'business schools', 'the business community', 'business people').

The significance of this pattern of collocations is highlighted by a very different one which Blair quotes in one of his speeches: 'When people say "keep business out of schools" I say … '. He doesn't identify who the 'people' are, but this is recognisably the sort of thing some people on the left would say, and it evokes left discourses in which government is constructed as in tension with and limiting or controlling business rather than, as in New Labour, just being in partnership with it and helping it. In the earlier Labour corpus there are 15 instances of 'business', of which 3 imply such tension: 'uncoordinated selfish business decisions directed to private profit', people as 'the manipulated digits of an impersonal business society', and 'regulation of big business and finance'. The others are more evaluatively neutral (e.g. 'gone our of business', 'Business education'). Neither the partnership nor the helping collocations of New Labour occur.

Competition and cooperation

The two main processes that nation-states are represented as involved in within the global order are 'competition' and 'cooperation' – the latter is also referred to by Tony Blair[7] as 'global partnership' ('partnership' is a New Labour keyword I discuss later) and a 'new internationalism' which is contrasted with 'narrow nationalism' and 'isolationism'. The latter are attributed to the Conservative Party because of the growth of anti-European Union sentiment. 'Cooperation' is represented as a necessary response to 'problems which cross borders', and it includes support for the economic institutions of globalisation in its current neo-liberal form (the IMF, the World Bank, etc.), as well as international peace-keeping and other forms of trouble-shooting, international management of environmental risk, and so forth. (In his Fabian pamphlet[8] on the 'Third Way' Blair lists: 'the management of trade, finance, the peaceful resolution of disputes, swift responses to pressing new problems, like the crises in Asia and Russia and the threat to the global environment'.)

Although New Labour represents competition and cooperation as complementary aspects of the new global order, there are apparent contradictions. Accounts of the global economy as a field of competition between nation-states construct the latter as subject to abstract processes of 'change' which they cannot control – in Blair's words,[9] 'how do we cope with these massive changes being thrust upon us?' By contrast, accounts of international cooperation construct nation-states as jointly managing and in control of the global economy. In the same speech, cooperation is constructed in terms of 'partnership' and 'rights and responsibilities': 'The developed world has a responsibility to transfer resources, expertise and assistance to the developing world. The developing world has a right to expect this but also a responsibility to ensure that resources are used productively and for the benefit of the poor.' Nation-states are constructed here as rational agents acting in moral ways. The contrast underscores the observation I made above: that abstract and externally imposed 'change' is partly the result of decisions made by governments as well as businesses.

The 'new internationalism' is consistently identified by Blair as one of the constituents of the 'Third Way' – for instance in his speech to the South African Parliament[10] he glosses the 'Third Way' as: 'It requires a different way in which we approach the economy with a different role of Government; it requires an altered concept of what a civic society means; it requires us to alter the way that Government itself works; and finally, the "Third Way" is not just about what happens in our countries, it is about our relations with the outside world.' Perhaps the clearest formulation of how 'internationalism' figures as part of the 'Third Way' was given in Blair's speech in Chicago in April 1999 on the eve of the NATO 50th anniversary meeting in Washington, and in the midst of NATO's air attacks on Yugoslavia.[11]

Metaphor

I commented earlier on the metaphorical character of the construction of 'change' in Blair's 'Confederation of British Industry' speech –

including 'change' being metaphorised as a tidal wave ('change that sweeps the world') or the mere passage of time ('trying to keep the clock from turning'), implying that change is inevitable and irresistible. There are always alternative possible metaphors available (one might for instance metaphorise change as tyranny or forcing people into a straitjacket), and the choice of metaphors contributes profoundly to meaning. The way New Labour represents relations between nation-states within the global order is itself metaphorical: representing relations between nation-states as 'competition' or 'cooperation' is implicitly claiming that they are rather similar to relations between individuals or organisations on a smaller scale (such as businesses or schools). It is far from obvious that this is so. Also, the contrast I pointed to above between the way competition is constructed and the way cooperation is constructed involves differences in metaphor: metaphors that imply the inevitability and irresistibility of change (e.g. the tidal wave, but also imposition by an all-powerful but unspecified agent – 'changes being thrust upon us') predominate when the theme is competition between nation-states, whereas when the theme is international cooperation the predominant metaphors construct nation-states as individuals working out their relations in mature and civilised ways (e.g. acknowledging – as we all should! – that rights go with responsibilities).

Enterprise culture

The equivalence between country, nation, and business goes with a positive construction of business. Some commentators suggest that New Labour is fascinated with the glamour of business.[12] The 'enterprise culture' was a central theme of the Thatcher Government in the 1980s.[13] It seems that New Labour is taking over Thatcherite discourse in this as in other respects. In his speech to the South African Parliament in January 1999, Tony Blair said that 'we need [a] culture of enterprise', and the White Paper on competition calls for an 'enterprise culture' and an 'entrepreneurial culture'.[14] The general idea that governments should seek social change through shifting 'culture' (implying an engineering of people's cultures from above) has been taken over from the Tories, as too has the glorification of 'enterprise' (one chapter of 'Our Competitive Future' is devoted to 'entrepreneurship'). Tory initiatives to develop 'entrepreneurial skills' in school children are also being extended.

In his press statement on the publication of 'Our Competitive Future', Peter Mandelson writes: 'Then (in the industrial evolution) we led the world in enterprise. Entrepreneurs harnessed the opportunities that came with mechanisation to produce world-beating goods'. In this 'one-nation' discourse there is no reference to the role of the industrial working class in this British supremacy or the price they paid for it. Calling industry or business 'enterprise' is a sort of semantic engineering, engineering of meaning – it seeks to attach the values of 'being enterprising' (taking initiatives, being creative, etc.) to a process that also has a less rosy aspect.[15] There is also an attempt to re-value 'entrepreneur' – to encourage its use in such positive senses.

The national community and civic society

The representation of the global economy as competition between nation-states leads on as I have said to a priority for government: making Britain more competitive. The focus is upon Britain as a whole, as a national community. The divisions and inequalities that have been the primary reference point for centre-left politics in the past virtually disappear – as do the trade unions. My concern in this section is: How is this effected in the language of New Labour?

'One nation'

There is an explicit commitment to 'one-nation politics', to a politics oriented to 'the needs of the whole nation', and specific measures designed to strengthen the 'national community' and its 'shared values'[16] (the quotations are from Blair's speech to the CBI). New Labour has taken 'one nation' from the political discourse of Conservatism at a point when the Conservative Party abandoned it in favour of the divisiveness of Thatcherism. The political discourse of New Labour is inclusive and consensual – it tries to include everyone, there are no sharp internal divisions, no 'us' versus 'them', no enemies. However, this may change: in the wake of the NATO attack on Yugoslavia (where Milosevic certainly was constructed as the enemy), Blair made quite a sharp attack on public service workers (see chapter 4).

There is an important step – perhaps the crucial step – in the logic of the 'Third Way'. It provides a basis for this inclusive politics: the claim that the policies that are needed for 'enterprise', for strengthening the competitiveness of British business, are also precisely the policies that are needed for 'fairness', for 'social justice'. Indeed, the argument goes a step further: success in enterprise depends upon a more just society (see below). Let me refer to an early formulation of this claim by Gordon Brown, the Chancellor of the Exchequer in the New Labour Government:[17] 'Fairness and efficiency can be simultaneously achieved if, and only if, we attack these evils (persistent unemployment, inadequate investment in skills, entrenched in-work poverty and discrimination in work) at their source by giving people the analytical and vocational skills ... to enhance their own value.' The key policy area for simultaneously achieving fairness and efficiency is education – its importance in New Labour policy is famously signalled in Tony Blair's frequently repeated slogan 'education, education, education'.

The representation of the global economy as a field of intensifying competition for survival between nation-states not only entails a focus on national unity rather than division, it also leads to elements of nationalist discourse in, for instance, the commitment to 'national renewal' and to Britain being 'the best', appeals to the 'British spirit', and to 'our destiny as one of the great nations of the world'.[18] These accord for instance with the distribution of union jacks by the Labour Party to supporters in Downing Street when Blair first arrived there as Prime Minister after the 1997 election.

Who are 'we'?

Part of what distinguishes one political discourse from another is how collective identities are constructed – what lines are drawn within the body politic, who is included and who is excluded, who a party claims to speak for, who it speaks against. There is always therefore a question about who the 'we' is (and therefore how the pronoun 'we' is used). In New Labour discourse 'we' is used in two main ways: sometimes it is used 'exclusively' to refer to the Government ('we are committed to one-nation politics'), and sometimes it is used 'inclusively' to refer to Britain, or the British people as a whole ('we must be the best'). But things are not so neat. There is a constant ambivalence and slippage between exclusive and inclusive 'we' – the pronoun can be taken as reference to the Government or to Britain (or the British). For instance: 'we intend to make Britain the best educated and skilled nation in the western world ... This is an aim we can achieve, if we make it a central national purpose to do it.'[19] The first 'we' is the Government – the reference is to what the Government intends. But the second and third 'we' are ambivalent – they can be taken either exclusively or inclusively. This ambivalence is politically advantageous for a government that wants to represent itself as speaking for the whole nation (though not only for New Labour – playing on the ambivalence of 'we' is commonplace in politics, and is another point of continuity with the discourse of Thatcherism).

There is often a vagueness about who exactly 'inclusive we' includes, for instance in: 'If Britain is to succeed in the new world marketplace, it has no future as a low-skill, low-quality, low-value, low-wage economy. To be competitive, we have to aim high.'[20] Notice again the equivalence of 'Britain' and 'we' which is implicit in the substitution of the latter for the former in the second sentence. Who is the 'we' here? Perhaps those involved in the British economy? But then isn't it only those who control the economy, in conjunction with those who control the state, who set 'aims'? Yet such a narrow interpretation of the 'we' is at odds with: 'This is a challenge for all of us. Taking responsibility to improve our country's performance. Tackling the gap in our performance by doing something ourselves to close it.' But does the 'we' really include 'all of us' – what about the young, the sick, the retired, the unemployed? The apparent inclusiveness of the language is at the expense of a vagueness that obfuscates difference.

In some cases there are problems in sustaining an inclusive discourse and avoiding divisions. The following extract is a case in point:

> Private sector income growth gives serious cause for concern. It would be the worst of short-termism now to pay ourselves more today at the cost of higher interest rates, fewer jobs. ... It is really up to us: the greater the responsibility, the bigger the reward. We have learnt that lesson so often in the past. We cannot afford to learn it again.[21]
>
> (Tony Blair, CBI speech)

This is again an inclusive 'we', yet the first sentence makes it clear that its inclusiveness is limited – Blair was referring to the private sector at a time when the income gap between private and public sector employment was growing. But what is really problematic in this case for the inclusive discourse is the irony of Blair addressing those (in the CBI) who literally 'pay themselves' (determine rates of pay, including their own) and have notoriously paid themselves considerably 'more' in recent years (the income gap between senior managers and the rest is also growing), while presumably referring to the mere aspiration of the generality of private sector employees for more pay (it is only in a figurative sense that they can 'pay themselves more'). The example illustrates the difficulty in sustaining an inclusive political discourse in a divided society – the obfuscation of divisions and antagonisms in such discourse may become more than obvious to people given the right circumstances.

But the language is not always and everywhere so inclusive, and the exceptions are worth noting. For example: 'We must end the deepening culture of a group of people, especially our youth, left out of the mainstream of society.'[22] Whereas in the example in the previous paragraph an inclusive 'we' obfuscates the difference between private and public sectors and between senior managers and the rest, in this case 'a group of people' including 'our youth' is set in opposition to 'we', with the implication that 'we' should take actions which affect them. It is possible to reword it inclusively to make it closer to the previous example so that the youth are represented as part of 'us': 'We must end the deepening culture of a group of people, especially youth, finding ourselves left out of mainstream society.' The point however is that there are significant distinctions within New Labour's apparently general inclusiveness.

The extract from Blair's CBI speech on pp. 25–6 shows a rather typical oscillation between personal and impersonal sentences, the former including both first person singular 'I' (as in the beginning of the first sentence, 'I believe in this country … ') and first person plural 'we' (as in the second sentence, 'We all know this is a world of dramatic change.'). Most of the impersonal sentences are statements about what is or is not the case (e.g. 'This is simply a recognition of the challenge the modern world poses.'), though there are also a number of sentences that just consist of lists of phrases (e.g. the third and fourth sentences, from 'In technology … '). The personal sentences add understandings of, feelings about, and interpretations of what is or is not the case (through the verbs 'believe', 'know', 'talk', and 'mean', and the adjective 'proud'). Blair thus shifts between speaking impersonally, speaking personally in the sense of on his own behalf, and speaking on behalf of 'us'.

Community and civic society

I have referred to certain continuities between the political discourse of Thatcherism and the new right and the political discourse of New Labour. But there is one element in the latter and especially in Tony Blair's language that differentiates it from Thatcherite as well as 'old Labour' language – communitarian discourse. Tony Blair has been heavily influenced by the communitarian philosophy of John Macmurray – basically the idea that individuals are created through their relationship to others in families and communities.[23] Macmurray combines Christian socialism and a conservative critique of the individualistic worldview of liberalism,[24] and it is this combination that has given Blair a distinctive political position and a basis for critiquing the neo-liberalism of Thatcher. The combination of this discourse with the conservative discourse of 'one nation' is an important part of the 'Third Way' – linked commitments to 'national renewal' and the 'strengthening of communities' (including families). The keyword 'community' no longer means what it used to mean for Labour – for instance, 'responsibility to the community' twenty years ago would most immediately be interpreted as referring to the responsibility of business, now its most immediate interpretation is referring to the responsibilities of individuals. The point is that 'community' has come to be understood in moral terms which emphasise that 'responsibilities' are the other side of 'rights'.

The following is an extract from a speech which Tony Blair gave to the South African Parliament in January 1999:[25]

the Third Way needs a concept of a modern civic society that is founded on opportunity and responsibility, rights and duties going together. Society has a duty to its citizens and its citizens have a duty to society. Hence, the New Deal in Britain where youth unemployment has gone down by over 30 per cent. ...

But – and here is the deal that is at the heart of a good, decent, modern civic society – in return for that opportunity we are entitled to demand law-abiding behaviour. We, for example, are cracking down on youth offenders, penalties for violent crime are being increased. I think the slogan 'Tough on crime, tough on the causes of crime!' was a slogan you used here as well as we did back in Britain. ...

We believe, therefore, in this concept of a strong, modern civic society and we can be equally fierce in our defence of racial and religious tolerance as in our attack on crime and social disintegration. What our people are looking for today is a country free from prejudice but not free from rules. They want a strong society bound by strong rules. That society should be fair and it should give the equality of opportunity that people need but it should also demand that responsibility back from them as citizens of that society.

The strengthening of communities is regularly linked to the strengthening of 'civic society' (or 'civil society') as in this extract. It illustrates not only the moral discourse that is a significant element in the political discourse of New Labour, but also its tendency to be linked with other discourses, including an authoritarian discourse. With respect to the moral discourse, we find in the discourse of New Labour moral claims (such as 'Society has a duty to its citizens, and its citizens have a duty to society.'), which are a novel addition to the recent political discourse of the centre-left. A number of terms are used in antithesis with 'rights', including 'responsibilities', 'duties' (both in the extract) as well as 'obligations'. The proliferation of terms (what we might call 'over-wording') is noteworthy in itself – it indicates that this is a major preoccupation for New Labour. (But the terms differ in their relative moral weight, and my impression is that the most morally loaded term, 'duties', is increasingly being used, although probably 'responsibilities' (which has legal as well as moral connotations) is still the most common).

Moral discourse is combined with contractual discourse which interprets the distribution of rights and responsibilities metaphorically as a 'contract' or 'deal' between the individual and society (the community) or the individual and government. New Labour has taken the expression 'New Deal' from the presidency of Theodor Roosevelt in the USA and launched a whole series of 'new deals'. The metaphor of the 'deal' (in contrast with that of the 'contract') is widely used in everyday language, and giving it such salience in their discourse is an effective populist move on the part of New Labour. Earlier in the same speech, Blair says 'our welfare system must provide help for those who need it but the deal that we are trying to create in Britain today is something for something. If we provide job opportunities we expect people to take them.' The expression 'something for something' is an echo and reworking of 'something for nothing', which alludes to right-wing critiques of benefit claimants as 'spongers' (see the *Daily Mail* headline in the next paragraph). The principle of 'something for something' is extended by New Labour to making all government finance conditional – for instance, public sector pay increases: in Blair's words again, 'yes, we recognise that we need to reward teachers and nurses properly but in return they must be prepared to embrace fundamental reform in the way they work'. Or as Gordon Brown put it in his speech on the Government's spending review in July 1998,[26] 'all new resources should be conditional on the implementation of essential reforms: money, but only in return for modernisation'. ('Modernisation' represents highly contentious changes such as welfare reform as if they were purely technical and value-free updatings.) Of course, the metaphor of the 'deal' is not the only conceivable one for such conditionality – another would be 'blackmail'!

The moral and contractual discourse of New Labour is an individualist discourse, which stands in contrast with the traditional collectivism of the centre-left and the left. The 'deals' that are contracted are primarily envisaged as deals which individuals enter into, the 'responsibilities' and 'duties' are primarily those of individuals. New Labour has abandoned even a residual orientation to collectivism and to social class.

Rights, responsibilities, and duties

The word 'rights' occurs a total of 114 times. Of these, 39 are in the collocation 'human rights', and a further 28 occur in other fixed expressions such as 'basic rights', 'civil rights', or 'democratic rights'. There are 13 occurrences in the collocation 'the rights of' (in one case 'to') followed by a phrase identifying a particular social group, e.g. 'the rights of ethnic minorities'. Of the remaining 34 instances where 'rights' occurs without such specification, 16 collocate with 'responsibilities' or 'responsibility' (e.g. 'a strong civic society must be based on responsibilities as well as rights') and 8 collocate with 'duties' (e.g. 'our welfare system is being redesigned around rights and duties'). That is, except where 'rights' is specified, there is a high probability in the language of New Labour that it will collocate with 'responsibilities' or 'duties'. In Blair's words, 'rights and responsibilities go hand in hand' in the politics of New Labour.

If we turn the relationship around and look at the word 'responsibilities', there are a total of 34 occurrences of which 14 collocate with 'rights', one with 'stake' ('everyone has a stake in society and owes responsibilities to it'), one with 'powers' ('we will increase the powers and responsibilities of parents'), and one with 'opportunities' ('where the opportunities we have are matched by the responsibilities we owe to the community'). This suggests a 50 per cent probability that 'responsibilities' will collocate with 'rights' or some equivalent expression on what Blair has called the 'something for some-thing' principle. In the case of 'duties' the probability is much higher: the word only occurs (a total of 8 times) in collocation with 'rights'.

By contrast 'responsibilities' in the earlier Labour corpus (30 instances) includes just two collocations with 'rights', one of which could be New Labour ('individuals have responsibili-ties to each other as well as rights', dating back to 1982), whereas the other relates to 'new rights and responsibilities' in industrial relations. 12 examples allude to responsibilities of public authorities (in collocations like 'executive responsibili-ties', 'responsibilities of local councils'), 2 to the community's 'responsibilities to its members' and 1 to the 'pastoral respon-sibilities' of teachers. In 2 more examples the 'responsibilities of governments' are represented as including (in one wording) 'maintenance of high and stable levels of employment'. There are 4 cases of 'sharing responsibilities' in family contexts between women and men, and 2 of 'family responsibilities'. 2 examples refer to 'responsibilities of the better off' towards others, and 1 to 'employers' responsibilities towards the disabled'. Finally, 3 examples refer to Britain's 'international responsibilities'. Summing up, the close relationship between 'rights' and 'responsibilities' in New Labour language is absent, and we have rather the divorcing of rights from responsibilities (it is largely corporate entities that have responsibilities towards individuals), which New Labour criti-cises in its forebears.

The moral discourse also slides into authoritarian discourse, and as so often the example given in the extract is about crime and espe-cially youth crime. The authoritarianism of Blair's famous and much-quoted slogan (also quoted by him here) 'Tough on crime, tough on the causes of crime!' was crucial in persuading sections of the middle class to trust New Labour.[27] The slogan was actually invented in 1993 by Gordon Brown, but reflects the thinking of both Blair and Brown after a visit to the USA from which they returned deeply impressed with Clinton and the New Democrats.[28] The word 'tough' occurs pervasively in New Labour language, and is another important populist element. For instance, on the day when the Welfare Reform Bill was published (10 February 1999), Tony Blair provided an exclusive article for the *Daily Mail*[29] under the headline 'It Really Is the End of the Something for Nothing Days', and predictably it includes: 'It's tough, but it's the right thing to do.' 'Toughness' permeates the article, from the stern and determined photograph of Blair to the wording of the 'powerful new signals we are sending': 'If you can work, you should work.', 'Those who are dishonest will not get benefits.', 'If you can save, you have a duty to do so.' This is a new authoritarian language. The *Daily Mail* obligingly echoes the Government's 'toughness' in its own lead story under the headline 'Welfare: the Crackdown', which refers to a 'tough new welfare regime' taking a 'tough line on incapacity benefit'.

There are also other authoritarian elements in the extract above. The verb 'crack down on' connotes firmly exercised authority, as does 'demand', while referring to people's responsibilities in terms of their 'behaviour' evokes the control of its inmates on the part of a penal or other disciplinary organisation (e.g. a prison or school). It is not entirely clear who the 'we' is here, but the centre-left has certainly not represented governments as 'demanding' particular 'behaviour' from citizens – in fact this language means they are no longer constructed as citizens but as subjects. (The last sentence of the extract strikes me accordingly as an odd mixture of civil and disciplinary discourse in collocating – combining – 'demand' with 'citizens'.) Finally, the language of disciplinary organisations is again evoked in the reference to 'rules'.

The family

The strengthening of community entails for New Labour the strengthening of the family – the link between the two is made explicit in the following extract from a speech Blair gave in the campaign for the Labour Party leadership in 1994:[30]

> The break-up of family and community bonds is intimately linked to the breakdown of law and order. Both family and community rely on notions of mutual respect and duty. It is in the family that we first learn to negotiate the boundaries of acceptable conduct and to recognise that we owe responsibilities to others as well as ourselves. We then build out

from that family base to the community and beyond that to society as a whole. The values of a decent society are in many ways the values of the family unit, which is why helping to re-establish good family life and community life should be a central objective of government policy, and cannot be done without policies, especially in respect of employment and education, that improve society as a whole. We do not show our children respect or act responsibly to them if we fail to provide them with the opportunities they need, with a stake in the society in which they live. Equally, we demand that respect and responsibility from them in return.

What is interesting here is that in his concern to establish the continuity between family and community, Blair represents the family as a sort of public space – he constructs the family through a discourse that is more usually applied to public institutions such as schools, representing family life in a formal and distanced way by emptying it of its intimacy through applying to it public categories such as 'mutual respect' and 'acceptable conduct'.

The 'Third Way'

I suggested above that the most crucial step in constructing the logic of the 'Third Way' is the claim that, in a knowledge-based economy, the action that is needed to make Britain (British business) more competitive in the global market is also the action that is needed for greater social justice. The demands of 'enterprise' are claimed to come together happily with the demands of 'fairness', which seems like an updated formulation of a famous and indeed notorious slogan from the earlier part of the twentieth century: 'what's good for Ford is good for America'. Actually, the claim goes rather further: it is that successful 'enterprise' in a knowledge-based economy depends on 'fairness' in the sense that it is those countries whose whole popula-tions are highly educated and skilled that will succeed best. When the 'Third Way' is summed up by Blair and others, it is usually in terms of the convergence of 'enterprise' and 'fairness' (or other equivalent terms): 'A belief in social justice and economic dynamism, ambition and compassion, fairness and enterprise going together'; 'The third way seeks to combine enterprise and fairness'.[31]

The 'Third Way' is a political discourse built out of elements from other political discourses, of the left and of the right. 'Enterprise' is as

I said above a new right, Thatcherite term, whereas 'social justice' belongs to social democratic discourse. But although the 'Third Way' is often represented by New Labour as bringing together elements from these two political discourses, it is not as simple as that. In particular there is a covert revision of what is on this account the social democratic side of the combination. For example, 'fairness' belongs as much to traditional (pre-Thatcherite, pre-neo-liberal) conservative discourse as to social democratic discourse, in contrast to 'equality' (which is not itself a part of New Labour discourse, though 'equality of opportunity' is).

The 'Third Way' is pervasively represented in the discourse of New Labour as reconciling 'themes' which have been seen as irrec-oncilable. Here is one of many formulations that begins with an explicit statement of this. It comes from Tony Blair's Fabian pamphlet[32] on the 'Third Way' (recall that I discussed another formu-lation in the Introduction):

> My vision for the 21st century is of a popular politics reconciling themes which in the past have wrongly been regarded as antagonistic – patriotism *and* internationalism; rights *and* responsibilities; the promotion of enterprise *and* the attack on poverty and discrimination. ... In New Labour's first year of government we have started to put the Third Way into practice. Cutting corporation tax to help business *and* introducing a minimum wage to help the lowest paid. Financial independence for the Bank of England *and* the biggest ever programme to tackle structural unemployment. New investment and reforms in our schools to give young people the skills they need *and* cracking down hard on juvenile crime to create secure communities. Reforming central government to give it greater strategic capacity *and* devolving power to bring it closer to people. Significant extra resources into priority areas such as health and education *and* tough and prudent limits on overall government spending. Investment *and* reform in the public sector. A key player in the EU *and* hostile to unnecessary centralisation.

'Patriotism', 'responsibilities', and 'enterprise' have belonged to the political discourses of the right; 'internationalism', 'rights', and 'attacking poverty and discrimination' to the political discourses of the left – though again the 'left' terms are not so simple, for 'internationalism' as I said earlier is used by Blair for international coopera-tion between states rather than in its traditional left sense of international labour movement solidarity. The meaning 'not only but also' is pervasively used in formulations of the 'Third Way', in a variety of expressions – in this case a stressed *and* (marked by italics), but other expressions include *as well as*, *yet also*, and so forth ('fairness *and* enterprise', 'fairness *as well as* enterprise', 'fairness *yet also* enter-prise'). Such expressions draw attention to assumed incompatibilities while at the same time denying them – they go against the expecta-tions of audiences or readers, they elicit surprise.

How are we to understand the aspiration to 'reconcile themes which in the past have wrongly been regarded as antagonistic'? A relatively modest interpretation would be that New Labour has found a balance between contrary themes. But New Labour often makes the more radical claim of 'going beyond' such contrary themes, transcending them. It is one thing to say that there may be ways of reconciling for instance the promotion of enterprise and the attack on poverty and discrimination; it is quite another to say that the two 'themes' can no longer be in conflict. The former is perfectly conventional – Labour governments in the past have made such claims – the latter is not. The claim of New Labour to constitute a 'new politics' must be based on the latter.

The point however from a language perspective is that the contentious and sometimes frankly implausible nature of the more radical claim is offset by what we can call the rhetoric of the 'Third Way' (in one sense of 'rhetoric'). Formulations of the 'Third Way' are made up like the one above of lists of assumed irreconcil-ables reconciled. Not only does the focus on denying expectations and asserting surprising compatibilities defocus the question of how the 'themes' are actually to be reconciled, the lists also give the sense that quite different pairings of 'themes' are equivalent. For example, the 'antagonism' between rights and responsibilities is quite different from that between promoting enterprise and attacking poverty and discrimination – the former is a matter of definition and can be resolved by ensuring that rights are made conditional on responsibilities, the latter involves fundamental differences of interest such that, for instance, what benefits enter-prise might aggravate poverty or discrimination. Lists have the effect of obscuring important differences. On the other hand they can be rhetorically effective in persuading people through the abundance of examples. (Recall the discussion of lists and equiva-lences earlier in the chapter.)

The 'Third Way' is sometimes described as 'beyond left and right', as transcending old political divisions, but at other times it is described as 'traditional values in a modern setting' (in the words of John Prescott quoted in the Introduction), or in terms of a continuity of values and objectives but a change in the means of achieving them. Blair formulates it in these terms in his Fabian pamphlet:

> The Third Way stands for a modernised social democracy, passionate in its commitment to social justice and the goals of the centre-left, but flexible, innovative and forward-looking in the means to achieve them. It is founded on the values which have guided progressive politics for more than a century – democracy, liberty, justice, mutual obligation and internationalism.[33]

There is a certain vagueness and inconsistency about whether the reference is to values or objectives or goals (and whether these are the same thing), what the traditional values are, and whose tradition they belong to. In the same pamphlet, Blair gives another, somewhat different, list of values: 'equal worth, opportunity for all, responsibility, community'. And other lists appear elsewhere, for instance: 'fairness, justice, the equal worth and dignity of all', 'justice, liberty, equality of status, above all the belief that it is in a strong society of others that the needs of the individual are fulfilled'.[34] With respect to whose tradition, Blair refers to the objectives of 'the centre and centre-left' in much the same terms: they 'remain ... but the means of achieving them ... have to be fundamentally reconsidered'.[35] Elsewhere, 'the values we cherish' are the values of 'the international community' – 'liberty, the rule of law, human rights, and an open society'.[36] One traditional left value that is consistently omitted is 'equality' (though 'equality of opportunity' and 'equality of status' appear). Moreover, although some of the terms are the same, the meanings are different. I have already commented on shifts in the meaning of 'community' and 'internationalism'. The meaning of 'social justice' has also shifted through the omission of 'equality' in the sense of equality of outcomes (entailing redistribution of wealth), and its substitution by 'fairness' and 'inclusion'.[37]

Values

'Values' occurs 19 times on the 'earlier Labour' corpus. 6 of these relate to 'value' in an economic sense (e.g. 'we shall therefore increase child benefit to £7.25 at 1981–82 values'). Of the remaining 13, 4 occur in the collocation 'socialist values', 2 others in collocation with 'socialism' or 'Socialists', and 3 more in collocation with 'Labour' (totalling 9). The remaining 3 are: 'civilised values', 'political values' (of 'monetarism'), the 'values and ideals which will guide the nation', and the 'relative values' of standard English and other varieties of English. A striking feature of these examples is that in 8 out of 19 occurrences of 'values' the context is one of political antagonism – conflict between Labour and its political opponents. For example: 'underlying our objectives is a reassertion of Labour's principles and values. We reject the selfish, acquisitive doctrines of capitalism.'; 'it is based on a set of socialist values fundamentally opposed to those of the present government'. 'Values' is coordinated with 'principles' (twice), 'vision' and 'ideals'.

There are 64 instances of 'values' in the New Labour corpus, none of them in an economic sense (so all in the moral sense). In contrast with the 'earlier Labour' corpus, 'values' never collocates with 'socialist' and only once with 'Labour', and there are no contexts of political antagonism. The predominant context is rather 'change' – 'values' occurs 29 times in contexts of change, modernisation, or more specifically applying traditional values to the modern world (the latter in 8 cases, e.g. 'we have liberated these values from outdated dogma and doctrine, and we have applied these values to the modern world'). The collocation 'British values' occurs 4 times, and 'our values' 12 times. There is a certain ambivalence about 'our' that is foregrounded in the following example from the 1997 Labour Manifesto: 'New Labour is the political arm of none other than the British people as a whole. Our values are the same.' This equivalence between New

Labour and British values occurs once again: 'Our actions on exclusion reflect our values and those of the British people.' Whereas in the earlier Labour corpus 'values' differentiated parties and people, in the New Labour corpus the values of the Party are the values of the nation. The point is evident in the adjectives that modify 'values' in the New Labour corpus, where meanings of tradition and commonality predominate: 'basic' (twice), 'clear', 'common', 'decent', 'democratic', 'enduring' (twice), 'essential', '(the) right' (twice), 'shared' (twice), 'simple', 'strong', 'traditional' (3 times). Another formulation of traditional values is: 'The attitudes of this generation but the values of all generations.' Whose values are at issue is in many cases established by the context: most commonly those of Britain (9 times), the Government (7), the 'Third Way' (6), New Labour (5), the Commonwealth (4), the European Union (3).

In opposition, Tony Blair saw the development of a new politics as a matter of shifting the political 'dividing-lines' – rejecting the Tories' 'dividing-lines' and imposing new ones.[38] For example, 'the divide on the market is not that the right believes in it, and the left doesn't, but between the laissez-faire market approach of the right and the left's commitment to investment in industry and education ... On tax ... not between high and low taxes but rather fair and unfair'.[39] What Blair is doing here is what any political discourse does – imposing divisions on the world. We might say that a political vision is a division. The French sociologist Pierre Bourdieu describes such divisions as 'symbolic violence' – violence in the form of language.[40] What is violent about it? Well, take another characteristic statement of Blair's:[41] 'New Labour is neither old left nor new right' – the 'Third Way' transcends that division. But were 'old left' and 'new right' the *only* options? Is the New Labour 'Third Way' the *only* alternative? The new 'dividing-lines' are no different from the old ones in forcing false alternatives. As Labour MP Ken Livingstone put it in a review of a book on the 'Third Way' by another sociologist, Anthony Giddens, democratic socialism is another 'third way' which New Labour's 'dividing-lines' effectively bury.[42] That is symbolic violence.

As we saw above, the 'Third Way' assumes that enterprise (the global economy) can 'go with' social justice, and education is a prime example of their compatibility: 'education is not just the great liberator, it is critical to economic development'[43] – another example of New Labour's favoured 'not only but also'. One problem with 'not only but also' formulations is that they imply that both elements are given equal weight, whereas in practice this may be far from true. This is really the same point that I made earlier about lists, in discussing the 'cascade of change': constructing elements as equivalent hides hierarchical and asymmetrical relations between them. In the case of education, the emphasis is overwhelmingly on economic development. This becomes evident when we look at how education is represented – what discourses are drawn upon in representing education. Education Minister David Blunkett's foreword to the Green Paper 'The Learning Age' assembles a variety of different discourses around learning[44] – it is 'the key to prosperity' and 'human capital', but 'love of learning' also goes with 'an enquiring mind' and 'civilised society' and 'helps us fulfil our potential and opens doors to a love of music, art and literature'. Yet the 'human capital' discourse is overwhelmingly dominant – in Blunkett's words, 'investment in human capital will be the foundation for success in the knowledge-based global economy'. Like any corporation, the Government 'invests' for competitive advantage, and in a knowledge-based economy that primarily means investing in 'human and intellectual capital'. Marx was scathing in his critique of people being referred to as 'hands' in the nineteenth century – 'human capital' is the same reification of people within a different technology. Of course, the term is widely used in business and management discourse – but should that be a model for Labour? A recent study of the expression 'lifelong learning' in a large collection of British and EU documents[45] suggests a radical restructuring of the relationship between the domains (and languages) of the economy and education is in progress – learning is becoming specialised as the development of human capital, and it would seem that New Labour is 'buying into' that.

There is a danger of overstating the significance of the 'Third Way'. It is a concept that is not only highly contentious in its claims about political change (specifically, that the 'old' politics divides into the two 'ways' it suggests, and that it somehow transcends that division), but has also been very limited in its uptake – it belongs to a small group of professional politicians and academics, and has hardly caught the popular imagination. At the same time, there are some indications that it is becoming an internationally powerful mobilising concept for (in Blair's terms) governments of the 'centre, centre-left'.

Really we have to say that the jury is still out: the 'Third Way' may turn out to be a short-lived idea, or it may turn out to be of longer-term importance.

Conclusion

My concern in this chapter has been to show how the logic of New Labour is constructed in its political discourse. I shall develop this in chapter 2 by focusing on one part of the political discourse of the 'Third Way', the construction of 'social exclusion'. While this has the advantage of bringing out the coherence of the politics of the 'Third Way', its limitation is that it gives an overly rigid and static view – it can give the impression that the language of New Labour is clearly demarcated and stable. In fact it is a fluid, internally diverse and shifting language, and it is important to complement the account I have given in this chapter with an attempt to capture these properties. That is the aim of chapter 3.

2

THE LANGUAGE OF 'SOCIAL EXCLUSION'

New Labour's commitment to a 'one-nation' politics and to strengthening communities (see chapter 1) goes with a concern to achieve an 'inclusive' society with strong 'social cohesion'. Reducing 'social exclusion' is therefore a policy priority, a target both for the welfare-to-work programme (the 'New Deal') and for the Social Exclusion Unit that was set up in December 1997 as a unit within the Cabinet Office steered personally by the Prime Minister. The importance attached to this initiative is evident from the claim of Peter Mandelson that 'the government's success would be judged by its response to the crisis of social exclusion',[1] and Blair's statement that the SEU is 'an experiment in policy-making that is vital to the country's future'.[2]

The Social Exclusion Unit is designed to produce what Blair likes to call 'joined-up government' with respect to social exclusion – to ensure effective coordination between different government agencies and effective 'partnership' between government, local government, voluntary organisations, and business. The scale of social exclusion was defined when the Unit was set up in terms of the 5 million people who live in households where there are people of working age but no one in paid work, and the 3 million people who live on the 1,300 worst housing estates in Britain. In its first phase the Unit produced three reports on specific aspects of social exclusion: truancy and 'school exclusion', street living, and the worst housing estates.

The concept of 'social exclusion' is a relatively new one in Britain, and represents a shift from the previously dominant concept of 'poverty'. The concept of 'social exclusion' is used in the European Union, and its adoption in Britain is part of an EU harmonisation. It incorporates Britain into an established continental European and especially French focus on marginalisation as detachment from the moral order of society, as opposed to the Anglo-Saxon liberal view of marginalisation as not commanding sufficient resources to survive in the market.[3]

New Labour did not immediately settle on the concept of 'social exclusion'. Others were used in the months immediately after the 1997 election when this aspect of the political discourse of the 'Third Way' was in the process of formation (see chapter 3). Blair devoted his first speech as Prime Minister in June 1997 to this issue.[4] Various terms are used in this speech, including 'poverty' and 'disadvantage', but 'social exclusion' is not, and in fact the speech centres around a new concept that does not seem to have survived beyond this one occasion, 'the workless class', which accords with New Labour's view that paid work is the most effective remedy for social exclusion. The setting-up of the Social Exclusion Unit was announced in a speech in August to the Fabian Society by Peter Mandelson[5] in which two terms were dominant: 'social exclusion' and the 'underclass'. In Blair's speech in December 1997[6] neither the 'workless class' nor the 'underclass' figured – the dominant term was 'social exclusion', and that is true also for the first publication by the SEU itself in the same month,[7] and subsequent publications. Although the concept of the 'underclass' has ceased to be used, the behavioural and moral delinquency which it suggests has carried over into the construction of social exclusion.[8] (See below.)

New Labour texts regularly construct social exclusion as 'more than' poverty – in Mandelson's speech, 'This is about more than poverty and unemployment. It is about being cut off from what the rest of us regard as normal life'; or in Blair's speech[9] launching the Social Exclusion Unit:

> Social exclusion is about income but it is about more. It is about prospects and networks and life-chances. It's a very modern problem, and one that is more harmful to the individual, more damaging to self-esteem, more corrosive for society as a whole, more likely to be passed down from generation to generation, than material poverty.

Correspondingly, 'tackling' social exclusion in 'not just the redistribution of cash from rich to poor',[10] 'it has to go beyond changes to the rate of benefit'.[11] Taken literally, expressions such as 'more than x' and 'not just x' can be interpreted to mean 'x as well as y, z, etc.'. However, such formulations in practice set up an implicit antithesis: 'y, z, etc. rather than x'. Concretely, 'prospects and networks and life-chances' rather than 'material poverty'. Notice how this slippage from addition to antithesis takes place in the Blair extract just above. The first two sentences are addition: social exclusion is 'prospects and networks and life-chances' as well as 'income'. But in the third sentence social exclusion is in fact contrasted with 'material poverty' – it is more 'harmful' and so forth than 'material poverty'. Similarly, government action to 'tackle' social exclusion in practice takes other measures *instead of* increasing benefits, *instead of* redistribution. But the antitheses that are set up are false antitheses: they assume that a choice has to be made between the more immediate relief of poverty and longer-term measures to prevent poverty, as if it were impossible to do both at once.

Social exclusion is seen as (in Mandelson's terms) 'multiple deprivation', and a feature of the language is lists of problems such as 'rising poverty, unemployment, educational failure and crime'.[12] The Social Exclusion Unit's initial leaflet defines social exclusion as:

> a shorthand label for what can happen when individuals or areas suffer from a combination of linked problems such as unemployment, poor skills, low incomes, poor housing, high crime environments, bad health and family breakdown.

Problems which might in different discourses be differentiated and separated are here made equivalent, as just so many aspects of social exclusion. The various agencies involved in 'tackling' social exclusion are similarly listed and made equivalent, for instance: 'views from local authorities, business, voluntary organisations and other organisations/individuals with experience of dealing with exclusion'. There is a negative side to constructing problems and agencies as equivalent by listing them in this way – it dedifferentiates them, i.e. it reduces the differences between them. In doing so it excludes certain conceivable relationships between them, and hence certain meanings, which one would find in other discourses that do not set up such equivalences (recall that I made this point in chapter 1, in discussing the 'cascade of change', pp. 28–9). In this case, it excludes explanatory accounts of the relationship between problems and agencies, which might produce formulations such as 'unemployment causes family breakdown', or 'poor housing can result in bad health', or 'business creates unemployment'. Lists and equivalences favour a logic of appearances (we 'see' all these problems together, for instance on certain housing estates) rather than an explanatory logic which tries to go beneath appearances to find explanations, including cause/effect relations between different problems and agencies.

Social exclusion – condition or process?

Peter Townsend, a highly influential British professor (now emeritus) of social policy, recently explained his 'conversion' from a vocabulary of 'poverty' to 'social exclusion' on the grounds that it directs attention to the 'marginalised and excluded and to the potential instruments of their exclusion', and to 'external creation and control of need'.[13] Another recent paper[14] identifies two key features of the 'social exclusion' concept – its comprehensiveness (it includes material poverty but also much else) and its dynamic character (which is what Townsend is alluding to). But it goes on to note an ambivalence – 'social exclusion' can foreground either a process (some people being excluded by other people, or by for instance the restructuring of industries), or an outcome (the state of being excluded). In the language of New Labour, social exclusion is an outcome rather than a process – it is a condition people are in, not something that is done to them. Correspondingly, although lack of paid work is seen as the primary reason for social exclusion, there is no specification of economic processes or agents that are responsible for producing unemployment. This ties in with what I said in chapter 1 about the 'ghost in the machine' – the invisibility of the multinational corporations as economic agents.

In the first leaflet produced by the Social Exclusion Unit,[15] the verb *exclude* is used only once, whereas the nominalisation *exclusion* occurs fifteen times – this in itself suggests that the 'outcome' sense of social exclusion rather than the 'process' sense is predominant, because one effect of nominalisation is to background process and foreground outcome. This effect is linked to the fact that nominalisations tend to involve the omission of the subjects and objects of verbs, which specify who the agent is, who is affected, and so forth – it is possible to retain them in expressions like *the social exclusion of a large number of people by contemporary capitalism*, but rather unusual. In this leaflet it doesn't happen – the subjects and objects (hence agents and 'affecteds') of *exclude* are omitted when it is nominalised as *exclusion* (e.g. 'the purpose of the unit is to coordinate and improve Government action to reduce social exclusion').

But there are other textual clues which suggest a focus on the condition of social exclusion rather than the process. If we look at the verbs that have 'social exclusion' as their object – for instance, 'social exclusion' is the object of the verb 'reduce' in the example I have just quoted – the list is: 'reduce' (used twice), 'tackle', 'probe', and 'deal with'. One can 'deal with' either a condition or a process, but the other verbs usually take objects that represent a condition, not a process. Again, 'individuals and areas suffer from a combination of linked problems' which constitute social exclusion – people 'suffer from' illnesses, and the metaphor again suggests that social exclusion is condition rather than process. The verbs that have 'social exclusion' as their subjects also favour interpreting it as condition – it 'happens' in certain circumstances, it 'arises'. The point I am making is that the words which 'social exclusion' co-occurs with in the leaflet, its 'collocations', favour it being interpreted as condition rather than process. As well as the verbs it collocates with, this is true of its collocation with 'characteristics' and 'indicators' (e.g. 'the key characteristics of social exclusion'). A comparison will make the point clearer. It seems that in some European Union documents, 'social exclusion' is constructed more as a process than it is by New Labour. For instance, in the introduction and conclusion of a report on an EU conference on social exclusion in Spain in 1995,[16] the verbs which took 'social exclusion' as their object were 'reduce', 'combat' (eight times), and 'prevent'. Unlike 'reduce', 'prevent' implies that 'social exclusion' is a process (notice that one can 'prevent' but hardly 'reduce' certain people (or circumstances) excluding others). 'Combat' is ambiguous – one can 'combat' the condition or the process of social exclusion. Taking the comparison in a different direction by contrast, the language of New Labour is rather similar to the language of a publication on social exclusion by the think-tank Demos whose ex-director (Geoff Mulgan) has been credited with New Labour's initiative in 'tackling' social exclusion – for instance 'tackling' is a verb favoured by both, and more generally both construct social exclusion as condition rather than process.

Social exclusion and poverty

There is a total of 44 instances of the verb 'exclude' and the nominalisation 'exclusion'. The nominalisation accounts for 32 of these (in the collocation 'social exclusion', except in 3 cases), and the participle functioning as a noun ('the socially excluded') for 3, leaving just 9 cases where 'exclude' functions as a verb. 'Social exclusion' is the object of the following verbs: 'tackle' (5 instances), 'attack' (3), 'combat' (3), 'eliminate' (1), 'fight' (1). Two of these verbs ('tackle' and 'eliminate') imply that social exclusion is a condition rather than a process, while the rest are ambiguous – e.g. 'measures that directly combat social exclusion' might be interpreted either as measures to prevent it happening or to 'tackle' it as a condition. There is no verb (such as 'prevent') which unambiguously constructs social exclusion as a process. Whereas most instances of 'exclude/exclusion' relate to 'social exclusion', most instances of 'include/inclusion' do not: only 3 out of 79 instances do, all of them nominalisations (e.g. 'we maintain high levels of social inclusion based on values of community and social justice').

There are 83 instances of 'poverty'. There are striking differences as well as overlaps in collocations depending on whether the reference is to poverty in Britain (54) or to 'world poverty' (29). 'Poverty' occurs as object of the following verbs where the reference is to the UK: 'tackle' (9 instances), 'create', 'face', 'fight', 'prevent', 'reduce', 'relieve' (one instance each); and as object of these verbs where the reference is international: 'eradicate' (4 times), 'eliminate' (1), 'solve' (1), 'reduce' (4), 'combat' (3), 'tackle' (3). The most interesting difference is that the more radical aims (e.g. 'we want Britain to provide a lead in the international effort to eliminate poverty') apply to world poverty, but not to poverty in Britain. The one apparent exception is 'prevent', but the context makes it clear that there is no undertaking to end poverty: 'the welfare state exists to prevent poverty where possible and relieve poverty where necessary'). Blair's Beveridge lecture of 18 March 1999 (which was not included in the corpus) was widely seen as a radicalisation of the Government's approach to child poverty, and the language shows this: 'poverty' occurs twice as the object of the verb 'end', e.g. 'I will set out our historic aim that ours is the first generation to end child poverty for ever.' There is also a contrast between the global and national contexts in the words with which 'poverty' is coordinated: 'poverty and debt/injustice/underdevelopment' for the former, 'poverty and social exclusion/social division/unemployment/welfare dependency' in the case of the latter.

Discourses of exclusion and inclusion

According to Levitas,[17] there are three different discourses associated with social exclusion and inclusion, and different constructions of them contrast in terms of which discourses and combinations of discourses they privilege. The three discourses are a redistributionist discourse, which focuses on poverty and attempts to reduce poverty by redistributing wealth; a social integrationist discourse, which sees exclusion as primarily due to unemployment and inclusion as getting people into paid work; and a moral underclass discourse, which attributes exclusion to deficiencies in the culture of the excluded and inclusion as entailing cultural change. Levitas traces a shift away from the redistributionist discourse in the progressive development of the discourse of New Labour under the leadership of Neil Kinnock and John Smith, as well as Tony Blair. The New Labour discourse of social exclusion is a combination of the social integrationist discourse (the focus on shifting people from welfare to work) and moral underclass discourse. The combination is evident in the following extracts from a speech by Harriet Harman, then Minister for Social Security, at the opening of the Centre for the Analysis of Social Exclusion at the London School of Economics:[18]

> Work is central to the Government's attack on social exclusion. Work is the only route to sustained financial independence. But it is also much more. Work is not just about earning a living. It is a way of life ... Work helps to fulfil our aspirations – it is the key to independence, self-respect and opportunities for advancement ... Work brings a sense of order that is missing from the lives of many unemployed young men. ... [The socially excluded] and their families are trapped in dependency. They inhabit a parallel world where: income is derived from benefits, not work; where school is an option not a key to opportunity; and where the dominant influence on young people is the culture of the street, not the values that bind families and communities together. There are some estates in my constituency where: the common currency is the giro; where the black economy involves much more than moonlighting – it involves the twilight world of drugs; and where relentless anti-social behaviour grinds people down ...

Harman refers here to a 'parallel world' – what she is doing here is constructing a vision of two incompatible worlds. The world of work draws upon the social integrationist discourse, the 'parallel world' draws upon the moral underclass discourse. Moral language is relatively covert, but it is present. The two worlds are brought together in one sentence near the middle of the extract – 'Work brings a sense of order that is missing from the lives of many unemployed young men.' Harman might have said: 'Work brings a regularity which is not found in the lives of many unemployed young men.' By saying the sense of order is 'missing' she suggests a lack, by referring to a lack of a sense of 'order' she implies a morally reprehensible disorder, and by referring to a lack of a 'sense' of order she implicitly points to deficiencies in values and culture.

Work

There are 383 instance of 'work', of which 205 have to do with employment and unemployment. (The rest include the 'work' of the Government, what will or won't 'work', and so forth.) There are a number of relatively frequent meanings which are linked to 'welfare-to-work'. 'Welfare-to-work' itself occurs 19 times, and expressions referring to getting people 'into' or 'back to' work occur a total of 23 times, including 10 instances of the phrase 'off benefit (welfare) and into work' – e.g. 'we will get 250,000 young unemployed off benefit and into work'. (By contrast there are 7 instances of 'out of work' and one each of 'without work' and 'no prospect of work'). There are 6 instances of seeking or finding work ('seek', 'look for', 'find', 'get', 'take up'), and the expression 'ready for work' occurs once – 'they will be ready for work when referred to an employer'. Opportunities to work are referred to 9 times ('opportunities'(5), 'chances' (4)), and 'barriers to' or being 'denied' work once each. Differentiating between 'those who are able to work' or 'those who are unable to work' seems to be another focus (12 instances in all). There are 9 instances of 'desire', 'want' or being 'anxious' to work, and a total of 26 expressions which relate to encouraging or promoting work ('encourage' (7), 'reward' (4), 'promote' (2), 'stimulate' (1), 'work incentives' (6), 'make work pay' (4), 'make work attractive', and make the tax and benefit system 'more work-friendly'). The phrase 'work ethic' is used twice (e.g. 'rebuilding welfare around the work ethic'), and once reference to those given opportunities having 'an obligation to take work'. Summing up, these collocations suggest that work is predominantly constructed in terms of getting those who can work into work.

'The right to work' is rather a surprising collocation for New Labour, but in fact it does occur twice. However, it is used in both its occurrences specifically with reference to disabled people who 'want' or have been 'denied too long ... the right to work'. What is absent is the left concept of 'the right to work' as a general right entailing a responsibility on the part of the state to ensure the availability of jobs. In the 'earlier Labour' corpus by contrast, in which there are a total of 137 instances of 'work' linked to un/employment, 'right to work' occurs 10 times in this sense, and connected with that 'work for all' 3 times, and in one instance the Government should 'make sure that jobs are available for those who want to work'. Democracy at work is a focus ('democracy' or 'rights at work' occurs 6 times), as are equalising pay and conditions at work (a total of 10 expressions, some of which refer specifically to gender (in)equalities e.g. 'promoting equality of opportunity at work', 'equal pay for work of equal value') and 'fulfilment at work' (twice). Another major group of collocations links to health and safety at work (12 in total, e.g. 'improve statutory protection with respect to health and safety at work'). There are 8 expressions related to improving the balance between work and leisure or work and family (e.g. 'enable both sexes to better combine family and work responsibilities'), 4 to reducing time at work ('looking forward to a society in which we work less'), sharing it more evenly and taking time off for study. And in one instance: 'life is not only work'. The collocation 'out of work' occurs 10 times, mainly linked to improving benefits (see below), but in two instances in contexts which suggest Government responsibility to provide jobs (e.g. 'the Labour Government will aim to ensure that no-one is out of work for more than 12 months without receiving an offer of a job'). By contrast, expressions linked to getting people 'into' work ('encouraging' people to work, and so forth) which are so salient in the New Labour corpus are few in number (one reference to a programme to 'take as many as 160,000 people out of unemployment and into work', and another 'designed to help disabled people back into work') . By contrast there are three instances of the Labour slogan 'get Britain back to work' (which implies Government action to create jobs). 'Opportunities for work' occurs once, and 'looking for' or 'finding' work a total of 3 times. Adequacy of benefits for those in or out of work is thematised in 8 collocations (e.g. 'an adequate level of child support for those in work', 'improving benefits for those out of work'). Summing up, whereas the focus in New Labour is getting people off welfare and into work, in the earlier Labour corpus the focus is on improving conditions and relations in work and in the balance between work and other things, and lack of work is constructed in terms of the right to work and the obligation of Government to provide work.

Marquand[19] identifies a fault line running through New Labour's inclusive coalition and its project for social inclusion:

> The central fault line in modern post-industrial society is that between the winners and the losers in the global marketplace. The lion's share of the extraordinary productivity gains associated with the current capitalist renaissance has gone to the owners of capital, to a new techno-managerial elite and to a handful of stars in the increasingly global entertainment industries ... Confronting them are the losers: the anxious middle classes, threatened by proletarianisation; the increasingly casualised working class; and the burgeoning underclass. That fault line runs through the New Labour coalition. No project for social inclusion will work unless it captures some of the winners' gains and redirects them to the losers. The notion ... that the workfare state can

turn the trick all by itself, that a mixture of training, education and moral suasion can transform the entire society into
winners, and that this can be done at nil cost to those who
have already won, is an illusion ... the losers' interests are
bound to differ from those of the winners, and it is self-
deception to pretend otherwise.

In the absence of such a 'redirection', the project of 'social inclusion' looks like mere words (see chapter 6).

Cultural governance

The claimed cultural deficiencies of socially excluded people are the
basis for advocacy of interventions by Government to change
cultures. This is not a new idea – the Thatcher Government had
interventionist policies designed to create an 'enterprise culture', for
instance. But what we might call 'cultural governance' – governing by
shaping and changing the cultures of the public services, claimants
and the socially excluded, and the general population – seems to be a
more systematic part of government under New Labour. For
instance, the new Minister of Social Security who replaced Harriet
Harman in the summer of 1998, Alistair Darling, announced in
February 1999 an annual audit of Government action to combat
poverty. This is interesting in that it re-centres 'poverty' rather than
'social exclusion' – what seems to have been a rather temporary shift,
though perhaps a recurrent one as New Labour tries to handle the
tension between its 'traditional' core supporters and its move towards
the middle class. But it is also interesting in its explicit commitment
to cultural governance. The following is an extract from the press
release:

> The Social Security Secretary stressed that as part of the
> fight against poverty a radical change of culture –
> confronting attitudes and long-term dependency – is
> needed.
> 'We know too well the effect that years of unemployment
> or illness have on individuals. It demoralises. People come to
> expect nothing different. And, in turn, their children expect
> no better for themselves.'
> 'This is the poverty of expectation that we must tackle by
> changing attitudes, and making sure that people know what

help and opportunities are available to them', added Mr Darling.

Notice that the moral deficiency of the culture which needs changing is implicit in the language – 'dependency' is pervasively constructed in negative terms, and a similar evaluation is attached to people's expectations by constructing them in terms of 'poverty'. Moreover, the way Government action is worded – 'tackling', 'confronting' – also implies such negative evaluation.

I referred above to the influence of the think-tank Demos on the Government's 'social exclusion' policy. In a Demos publication[20] devoted to 'tackling social exclusion' (which incidentally makes frequent use of New Labour's favourite verb 'tackle'), social exclusion is seen as centrally involving 'cultures of low aspiration and fatalism', which 'encourage people to believe that low paid work will always be a dead end "McJob" or a fast route back to the dole'. Accordingly, 'tackling social exclusion means changing cultures', 'influencing the "cultural lenses" – aspirations, time horizons, attitudes to risk, and so on – through which socially excluded people perceive the incentives they face'.

The voice of the 'socially excluded'

A danger in focusing on the language of New Labour (or indeed any language which figures in a field of complex relationships with other languages) is that its social power tends to be overstated, because the ways in which it is taken up, resisted, or just ignored, are not in focus. I want to give a corrective, if a very partial one, at this point by giving voice to people who are in the New Labour sense socially excluded, and looking at how the language of New Labour is taken up in their language. The following includes three voices of people involved in 'fiddly jobs' in the north-east of England – people who are working while claiming social security benefits. This is illegal, and a central element in New Labour's welfare reform is combating such 'fraud'.

PHIL: There's enough around. All you have to do is to go into any pub or club, that's where the work is. The person you mentioned he probably just sits around watching the telly. To get a job round here you've got to go around and ask people.

DANNY: Most of it is who you know. You've got no chance of getting a job in the Job Centre. ... You go out to the pub. People who go to the pub go to work.

STEPHEN: He [the 'hirer and firer'] just shows his face in The Rose Tree or The Gate, and people jump and ask him for work. When I was working there I've seen him just drive off in his van around the pubs and he'll come back with another twenty men to work, an hour later. No one asks any questions.

It's a matter of us being cheaper. It's definitely easier than having a lot of lads taken on permanently. It would cost them more to put them on the books or pay them off. It's just the flexibility. You're just there for when the jobs come up, and he [the 'hirer and firer'] will come and get you when you're needed. You need to be on the dole to be able to do that. Otherwise you'd be sitting there for half the year with no work and no money at all.[21]

One focus of the Demos article I referred to earlier is on poverty in 'social capital' and social networks as a factor in social exclusion. But Jordan[22] has argued that the 'socially excluded' develop their own often effective social capital and social networks to survive. In fact, such social capital and social networks constitute the theme of the extract above. Notice also the proverb 'People who go to the pub go to work.' What is interesting about it is that it suggests the continuing power of proverbs (which are often seen as merely archaic) in formulating and transmitting knowledge (social capital) in everyday culture. Jordan also argues that the sort of survival strategies represented here are a perfectly rational – and in no reasonable sense criminal – response to the conditions in which people find themselves. They are based upon a perception of how the new form of capitalism works and a rationale for ways of acting in response to it, which is widely recognised in everyday life, but not within official public discourse. We can read Stephen here as giving a formulation of such a rationale: black labour is part of the 'flexibility' of the new capitalism, but it is so undependable that only people on social security ('the dole') can do it. Notice the word 'flexibility'. Stephen is giving voice to the neo-liberal economic discourse which New Labour has adopted. But there is a reversal: whereas New Labour tries to present tackling social exclusion as enhancing economic dynamism and hence flexibility, Stephen constructs social exclusion as an effect of flexibility. Whereas black labour services the system at one point, it causes problems at another because it gives people an alternative to moving from welfare into poorly paid work. Jordan's analysis sees 'tackling social exclusion' as an attack on the social networks of socially excluded people to force them into such jobs. If this is the case, there is an interest for Government in these voices and their logic being kept out of public debate.

What the example above indicates is the ways in which the 'socially excluded' themselves act in response to being excluded. In New Labour representations of social exclusion, by contrast, 'tackling' social exclusion involves the 'socially excluded' being acted upon especially by Government agencies rather than acting. However, the agency is rather more complex. It is up to Government to provide the 'opportunities' especially for education and training, people have the 'right' to such opportunities; but they also have the 'responsibility' to take up opportunities, to act to help themselves but only within the parameters set by Government. By contrast, a left discourse would tend to emphasise not only relations of agency and causality in the production of social exclusion, but also the agency of the 'socially excluded' (the poor, the oppressed) in struggling within and against those exploitative and exclusionary relations.

Conclusion

Why is New Labour committed to 'tackling' social exclusion? Characteristically, the rationales that New Labour politicians give combine morality with self-interest. I say 'characteristically' because one finds the same mix elsewhere – for instance, Blair described actions on the part of what he calls 'the international community' such as the NATO intervention in the Yugoslav Republic as 'guided by a … subtle blend of mutual self-interest and moral purpose … If we can establish and spread [our] values … then that is in our national interests too'.[23] Here is Blair talking in similar terms about social exclusion:

> Our actions on exclusion reflect our values and those of the British people. It offends against our values to see children with no prospect of work, families trapped in poverty, neighbourhoods blighted by crime.
>
> But this isn't just about compassion. It's also about self-interest. If we can shift resources from picking up the costs of problems to preventing them, there will be a dividend for everyone.
>
> We now have a chance for the first time in a generation to prevent Britain irretrievably sliding into division. A chance to bring Britain together.[24]

Once again, we have New Labour's favoured 'not only but also' ('this isn't just … it's also') relation, and as usual it is a problematic relation. In this case, the problem is knowing how much weight really attaches to compassion and values, and how much weight attaches to self-interest. (The same question arises with the Yugoslav war.) What this extract indicates is the fear which underlies policies to reduce social exclusion – the fear of an 'irretrievable slide into division'.

The long-standing Labour Party objective of greater equality has been displaced in New Labour by the objective of greater social inclusion.[25] The objective of equality in left politics has been based upon the claim that capitalist societies by their nature create inequalities and conflicting interests. The objective of social inclusion by contrast makes no such claim – by focusing upon those who are excluded from society and ways of including them, it shifts away from inequalities and conflicts of interests amongst those who are included, and presupposes that there is nothing inherently wrong with contemporary society as long as it is made more inclusive through government policies.

3

THE MAKING OF THE LANGUAGE OF NEW LABOUR

In this chapter I shall look at the language of New Labour 'in motion' so to speak – at the dynamics of New Labour's political discourse. I consider first the development of the political discourse of New Labour in its relationship to other political discourses both in Britain and internationally, including the political discourse of Thatcherism in Britain, the discourse of Clinton and the New Democrats in the USA, and political (including social democratic) discourse within the European Union. Although there are differences across this range of political discourses, there also appears to be a dynamic in the development of political discourses which they are all involved in and which transcends both national boundaries and traditional political divisions between left and right. What seems to be emerging is a new international political discourse of the centre-left – an international discourse of the 'Third Way'. It is worth noting in this connection that New Labour has been instrumental in setting up a series of international 'seminars' on the 'Third Way', attended not only by Blair and Clinton but also by leaders from other countries, including Brazil, Sweden, Italy, and more recently Germany. However, in so far as such a new political discourse is emerging, it seems to me to be a centre-left strain within neo-liberalism rather than an alternative or even serious corrective to it.

One important feature of this development is that it goes beyond politics and government to include, for instance, business, non-governmental organisations, and international agencies such as the World Bank and the International Monetary Fund. It is beyond the scope of this book to trace these connections in detail, but there do seem to be grounds for considering whether a new discourse is emerging across these organisations. This question is part of a broader one to do with shifts in the nature of governance, which I discuss in chapter 5: New Labour is committed (though in part only rhetorically) to a 'reinvention' of government. This involves giving more power to 'networks' or 'partnerships', which include all the various types of organisation to which I have just referred, and is in line with wider international developments in governance.[1] One way of putting this is in terms of the emergence of a powerful new complex of organisations (in the sense that the left used to refer to the 'military-industrial complex' in, for instance, the USA), which is partly a new discourse in common.

My second concern in this chapter is in a sense a corrective to the first. Despite the inclusive 'one-nation' discourse of New Labour, its mitigated version of neo-liberalism does not serve all interests equally: there are winners and there are losers, and there are consequently political differences which arise and which are constituted as differences in discourse. These differences are evident between political parties, including on the left between the Labour Party and other parties and groups, some of which are made up of former Labour Party members (such as the Socialist Labour Party associated particularly with the Miners' Union leader, Arthur Scargill). The differences are also evident within the Labour Party in divisions between supporters and opponents of New Labour, as well as within New Labour. I should also add that politics and government are complex and many faceted, and that this diversity (e.g. between the areas of social policy and foreign policy) itself entails diversity within political discourse. But the main point is that the convergences, to which I have referred in the above paragraphs, take place within a field of difference and contestation, which they can never eliminate though they may more or less succeed in marginalising. Moreover, critique of the language of New Labour is grounded in such differences and contestation, which is another reason for referring to them. See the discussion of critique of language in the Introduction and in chapter 6.

My final concern in the chapter is to represent the political discourse of New Labour as something which is changing and developing over time. This is partly a matter of showing contrasts between earlier and more recent New Labour discourse. It is also more fundamentally to do with how we see the documents, speeches, and interviews of New Labour. The basic question is this: Does language work expressively, or constitutively? In other words, does (for instance) a speech by Tony Blair simply give expression to a political position that was already worked out before and outside the speech? Or, on the contrary, does the speech actually constitute and produce a political position that will be certainly similar to positions in other

speeches, yet nevertheless distinct? I shall adopt the second, constitutive, view of political language, and illustrate it with reference to a
particular speech of Blair's. The ongoing constitutive work of political
language is framed and shaped by (and contributes to the framing
and shaping of) the shifting overall constitution of the
political/governmental field in its relations to other fields (e.g. business), nationally and internationally. That is to say, it is framed and
shaped by the convergences, differences, and contestation I have
referred to above.

New Labour and neo-liberalism

New Labour and the New Democrats

The victory of Bill Clinton and the New Democrats in the 1992 US
presidential election was a crucial external factor in shaping New
Labour – in strengthening the conviction of Blair, Brown, and others
in the need for the Labour Party to 'modernise' itself in order to win
power, to move towards the middle class and the political centre, and
to incorporate elements of the political themes and discourse of the
right and especially the new right.[2] Blair and Brown visited the USA
together in January 1993. According to Rentoul, the visit 'marked a
turning point in Blair's development as a politician'. It was not a
matter of Blair (or New Labour) borrowing piecemeal from the New
Democrats, but recognising similarities between the 'modernisers' in
the two parties and applying 'some of the Democrats' vivid language
to a body of ideas which he had already largely developed'. In particular 'Blair had at last found a populist language in which to express
the ethical socialist ideas which had formed his political
convictions.'[3] What these claims of Rentoul suggest is that the political discourse of New Labour was significantly shaped by what they
learnt from the New Democrats. As Rentoul points out, the traffic
has been two-way – e.g. Clinton took the theme of 'one nation' from
New Labour in his campaign for re-election in 1996, and has
recently used the term 'Third Way'.

My first concern in this section is to show that Clinton's political
discourse is indeed strikingly similar to Blair's. Both have selectively
assimilated elements of the discourse of the new right into new
political discourses that cannot however be simply seen as new right.
The politics and discourse of New Labour can appropriately be seen
as 'post-Thatcherite' in the sense that it does not seek to ground itself
in social democratic traditions which preceded Thatcher, but takes

Thatcherism as its starting point accepting elements of it while rejecting and seeking to go beyond others.[4] By the same token, the New Democrats might be called 'post-Reaganite'.

I shall refer to a book published by Bill Clinton in 1996, *Between Hope and History*. As in the discourse of New Labour, Clinton's political strategy is anchored in a representation of 'change' as an abstract, external and unquestionable process, which presents us with 'opportunities' as well as 'challenges', and which we must be prepared to 'embrace'. The discourse and rhetoric are similar to New Labour's:

> As we move from the Industrial Age into the Information Age, from the Cold War to the global village, the pace and scope of change is immense. Information, money and services can and do move around the world in the blink of an eye. There's more computing power in the Ford Taurus than there was in Apollo 11 when Neil Armstrong took it to the moon. By the time a child born today is old enough to read, over 100 million people will be on the Internet. Even our family cat, Socks, has his own home page on the World Wide Web. The opportunities this age presents us are extraordinary … But the challenges of this age are also extraordinary and the costs of failing to meet them is high.

The rhetorical figure I referred to in chapter 1 as the 'cascade of change' is prominent here as in New Labour, giving a sense of the inevitability of change (and the need therefore for radical change on the part of government), and favouring a logic of appearances rather than an explanatory logic (recall the discussion on p. 28). There is also the same elision of agency, causality, and responsibility when it comes to processes in the global economy – information, money, and services simply 'move around the world' apparently under their own steam, and there is no indication of social relations and responsibilities behind these movements.

Although Clinton does not use the expression the 'Third Way' in this book (he has used it elsewhere), he sees his own politics as going beyond the existing left and right alternatives, government 'spending more money on the same bureaucracies working in the same way' or government as 'inherently bad', to 'break out of yesterday's thinking and embark upon a new and bold course for the future'. 'A strategy', he goes on, 'rooted in three fundamental American values: ensuring that all citizens have the *opportunity* to make the most of their lives; expecting every citizen to shoulder the *responsibility* to seize that opportunity; and working together as a *community* to live up to all we can be as a nation.' The book is an elaboration of the three italicised themes of this strategy. In his Fabian Society pamphlet[5] on the 'Third Way', Blair writes: 'Our mission is to promote and reconcile the four values which are essential to a just society which maximises the freedom and potential of all our people – equal worth, opportunity for all, responsibility and community.' The 'new politics' for both Blair and Clinton involves a combination of the centre-left theme of equality of opportunity, the theme of responsibility which they have appropriated from the new right, and the theme of community which shows a shared orientation to communitarianism.

There are striking similarities in themes, in arguments, in particular policies, and in language. Both New Labour and the New Democrats advocate a role for government in equipping people to succeed in the global economy. In so doing, they distance themselves from the excessive reliance on market mechanisms and retreat from government of the new right governments that preceded them. In Clinton's words: 'We need government to do those things which are essential to giving us the tools we need to make the most of our lives.' At the same time, both advocate 'the reinvention of government', though for Clinton this prominently involves government being 'smaller' as well as 'more responsive' (I am focusing on similarities, but there are also of course significant differences). Both use the language of 'investment' with respect to education: government 'investing in education', 'investing in people'. And both use the same sort of strategy and language with respect to standards in schools:

> [W]e have worked hard to help them establish clear standards for what we expect out teachers to teach and our children to know, assess their performance in attaining those standards, and ensure accountability when they do not. ... Teachers must also demonstrate competence, and we should be prepared to reward the best ones and remove those who don't measure up fairly and expeditiously. In the same way we should reward the best schools and shut down or design those that fail.[6]

For both New Labour and the New Democrats 'freedom' or 'opportunity' or 'rights' must go with 'responsibility'. In Clinton's words: 'freedom works only when it is exercised with responsibility ... from the beginning [of the USA], opportunity and responsibility have gone hand in hand'. For both governments there has been a failure to accept responsibility, which they are committed to correcting – again in Clinton's words: 'so many of our social problems require people to reassert control over their own lives and to assume responsibility for their conduct and their obligations'. For both, welfare reform is framed in terms of the theme of responsibility. Both use the expression 'welfare-to-work' to focus what they see as the priority for a reformed welfare system. 'Moving people from welfare to work' is seen by both as 'moving people from dependence to independence and greater dignity' – both regard their existing welfare systems as the new right does, as 'trapping' people in 'dependency'; both see ending the cycle of welfare dependency in terms of people taking more 'responsibility' (all the quotations are from Clinton). Furthermore, both favour the word 'tough' – being 'tough on work and responsibility', as well as being 'tough' on crime.

In chapter 1 I quoted Tony Blair on the relationship between family and community (see pp. 42–3). Here is Clinton on the same theme:

> Today our 'yeoman farmers' are America's families. [Clinton is alluding to Thomas Jefferson's argument that the yeoman farmer was the bedrock of American democracy – people who 'hold a stake in, and take responsibility for, how our society works'.] The values they represent, the lessons they pass on to their children, the responsibility they take for shaping their own future, and the dreams they seek to achieve determine much about who we are as a people and what we can become as a nation. But families can be strong only if American democracy provides a climate in which they can thrive. Families can't be strong if they're mired in welfare. They can't be strong if the opportunity to earn a living and support their children is uncertain. They can't achieve economic security unless they have access to education. They can't be strong if the streets in their neighbourhoods are dangerous, if the environment is unsafe, or if events elsewhere in the world seem threatening.
>
> America has a stake in, and a responsibility for, strengthening families, the building blocks of our national community. Families, in turn, have a stake in and a responsibility for strengthening America. That process of strengthening, of taking responsibility, begins in the home, extends into the neighbourhood, grows out to the community, and creates a better America.

There is a close similarity between the two extracts in terms of main themes: the responsibility which is crucial to community at all levels develops first in the family; the values of the family affect the sort of society we have; families are under threat and need support from government. There are also similarities in the language – the key terms 'values', 'opportunities', 'responsibility', and 'community', but also the language of 'stakeholding' ('having a stake in' – I discuss this in some detail in the last section of this chapter). There are however differences both with respect to more specific themes (for instance the themes of unsafe environment and threatening events 'elsewhere' are absent from the Blair extract) and with respect to major themes: the theme of nation has a salience in the Clinton extract which is absent in the Blair extract, which refers to 'society as a whole' where Clinton refers to 'America'. Anticipating the concerns of the last section of this chapter, the two politicians produce, despite the common features, texts that articulate (substantially shared) political themes together in distinct ways. Blair and Clinton work similar themes and arguments into distinct (if still similar) political discourses.

New Labour and Thatcherism

I suggested above that New Labour is 'post-Thatcherite' – taking Thatcherism as its starting point and accepting certain elements of it while seeking to go beyond it in others. Although the discourse of New Labour is a new discourse, a new mix of elements, some of those elements are derived from the political discourse of Thatcherism. Here is an extract from a lecture given in July 1979 by Margaret Thatcher, shortly after her first election victory, which was entitled 'The renewal of Britain':[7]

> The mission of this Government is much more than the promotion of economic progress. It is to renew the spirit and the solidarity of the nation ... we need to inspire a new national mood, as much as to carry through legislation. At the heart of a new mood in the nation must be the recovery of our self-confidence and our self-respect. ...
>
> The foundation of this new confidence has to be individual responsibility. If people come to believe that the State, or their employer, or their union, owe them a living, and that, in turn, the world owes Britain a living, we shall have no confidence and no future. It must be quite clear that the

responsibility is on each of us to make the full use of our talents and to care for our families. It must be clear, too, that we have a responsibility to our country to make Britain respected and successful in the world.

The economic counterpart of these personal and national responsibilities is the working of the market economy in a free society. I am sure that there is wide acceptance in Britain going far beyond the supporters of our party, that production and distribution in our economy is best operated through free competition.

A basic function of Government is to ensure that this market remains in being. The Government must be responsible, too, for ensuring the maintenance of social cohesion ... Governments can purify the stagnant and corrupt parts of an economy and correct irregularities in the market, but they should not seek to regulate the market itself. Governments may provide certain goods and services which cannot easily be supplied competitively, but they should accept that one of their essential tasks is to define their limitations and those of the State.

... We need ... to create a mood where it is everywhere thought morally right for as many people as possible to acquire capital; not only because of the beneficial economic consequences, but because the possession of even a little capital encourages the virtues of self-reliance and responsibility, as well as assisting a spirit of freedom and independence.

The themes of national renewal, individual responsibility, maximising competition, and the limitations of government are all themes in New Labour discourse. On the other hand, the theme of spreading ownership of capital is not (though New Labour has accepted Conservative policies to practically encourage it). Another significant commonality however is the view that part of the business of government is 'creating moods' – or, in the more sociological language of New Labour, 'changing cultures' (though it was the Conservatives who launched the initiative of 'enterprise culture', which has also been taken up by New Labour). The Conservatives under Thatcher realised that their project for radical social change was best achieved through the relatively slow and patient groundwork of changing attitudes, moods, and cultures rather than head-on – through ideological means, and therefore through discourse. This is one respect in which New Labour has followed Thatcherism, and it is of particular interest here because it implies a language turn in politics – an enhanced salience for language in achieving social and political change.

Thatcher elaborates on the limitations of government and the state:

> It is certainly the duty of Government to do all it can to ensure that effective succour is given to those in need. Where Conservatives part company from Socialists is in the degree of confidence which we can place in the exclusive capacity of the Welfare State to relieve suffering and promote well-being. ... the collectivist ethos has made individuals excessively prone to rely on the State to provide for the well-being of their neighbours and indeed of themselves. There cannot be a welfare system in any satisfactory sense, which tends ... to break down personal responsibility and the sense of responsibility to family, neighbourhood and community.

This is reminiscent of the theme of 'rights-and-responsibilities going together' in New Labour, but also the theme of strengthening communities and civil society, and strengthening the family.

The commonality of themes is clear enough, as are certain thematic differences. And to a degree this is also a commonality of language, of political discourse. For instance, there are strong similarities between Thatcher and Blair in the representation of nation – both, for example, refer to the national 'spirit' ('the British spirit has always been able to rise to challenges'[8]). They also share a propensity to tough, populist language – Thatcher speaking of people believing that others 'owe them a living', Blair writing of ending the days of 'something for nothing'[9] and, of course, keywords such as 'responsibility'. But there are, at the same time, differences. One difference which I shall discuss in chapter 4 is that Thatcher's discourse is highly polemical and very much oriented to identifying enemies of her new right political project, dividing 'us' from 'them', whereas Blair's discourse is inclusive and consensual.

The European Union

There is little public recognition of the extent to which the policies, themes, and language of New Labour are also those of the European

Union. Significant elements of the political discourse of New Labour flow across national boundaries in Europe, as well as in many cases between Europe and other regions, including North America. For example, Piper[10] notes that the concept of 'human capital' and of educational expenditure as a form of 'investment' which developed in the early 1960s in the USA are now a central theme of European Union policy. For instance, the European Commission White Paper on education and training[11] proposes to 'treat material investment and investment in training on an equal basis'. Piper shows that both in the language of the European Union (1996 was the 'European Year of Lifelong Learning') and in the language of New Labour (as well as of the preceding Conservative government) 'lifelong learning' is a keyword which is part of economic rather than educational language – as if 'learning' had become an economic rather than an educational process.

The language of New Labour is conditioned and partly shaped by the requirement of giving national shape to European Union policies. A case in point is 'social exclusion'. As I pointed out earlier (see chapter 2), 'social exclusion' has largely replaced 'poverty' in the discourse of New Labour (though 'poverty' does periodically re-emerge as a focus). The direction of flow in this case is clearly from the European Union into Britain (in contrast, for example, to 'flexibility' where Britain under New Labour – like Britain under the Conservatives before them – is seeking to impose Anglo-American policies and language). But what is at issue is not simply the term 'social exclusion', but the language of policies oriented to social exclusion.

The standard view of 'social exclusion' in the European Union is summed up in the following extract from a report by the European Foundation for the Improvement of Living and Working Conditions:[12]

> Over the past 20 years, Europe has been facing an economic and social situation characterised by rapid, complex and profound change. While the majority of Europe's citizens have benefitted with increased opportunities and improved living and working conditions, a significant and growing minority have suffered poverty, unemployment and other forms of social and economic disadvantage ... that restrict their ability to cope with and master change. The longer these disadvantages persist, the wider becomes the gulf between those vulnerable to change and those who benefit from it.

This leads to two challenges for the European Union:

What can we do about the gulf which has appeared, and is widening, between those who benefit from change and those who do not?

How can we best support and assist those who have been adversely affected by change, both to cope with its effects upon them, and to turn it from threat to opportunity?

New Labour has taken on this view of social exclusion, and also policies to 'tackle social exclusion' and promote 'social cohesion' (the usual European Union word) or 'social inclusion' (the term New Labour prefers). The themes and, to some extent, the language of European Union social exclusion policy are also taken on by New Labour. For instance, the same publication gives a summary of 'common and consistent messages for policy-makers', which includes advocacy of an 'integrated approach to social, economic and environmental policy' (what Tony Blair calls 'joined-up government'), 'prevention is better than cure', improving the 'delivery' of services (which is 'more important than what they are'), encouraging the 'participation' of the people involved and 'local initiatives and community organisations', and forming 'partnerships for action', including government, business, trade unions (which tend to be ignored by New Labour), and voluntary and community organisations.

An international neo-liberal discourse?

A fundamental aspect of what makes New Labour 'new' is its abandonment of an economic role for the state – its assumption that it is faced with a 'new global economy' whose nature it cannot change and should not try to change. This is in contrast with social democratic and democratic socialist traditions, which have seen the state as having the capacity and the responsibility to modify the capitalist economy, notably through nationalisation and the formation of a 'mixed economy'. When the expression 'mixed economy' is used in a speech by Blair, it is used metaphorically to refer to 'partnerships' – 'we are building new public and private partnerships. There needs to be a mixed economy in the funding of welfare comprising the state, private and voluntary sectors.'[13] (Similarly, another term from the left tradition 'internationalism' is regularly used in a totally different sense – no longer for solidarity between workers, but for the sort of cooperation within the 'international community' which has led to NATO attacking Yugoslavia. See chapter 6.)

New Labour is not unique. Its abandonment of the 'economic state' is broadly shared by the social democratic parties, which constitute governments in most European Union countries at the time of writing, as well as the New Democrats in the USA. But so too is its strategy of containing and reducing the 'social state'. Although there are significant differences in detail, reform of welfare systems along broadly similar lines is on the agenda of all of these countries. At the same time, there is a common orientation to strengthening the 'penal state' – to 'tougher' government action against crime.[14]

One interpretation of these commonalities is that they constitute elements of an international neo-liberal politics: governments are accepting the globalisation of the economy and the neo-liberal argument that it entails a drastic revision and reduction of the welfare state, and adopting a punitive stance towards those who are the victims of economic change and of the retreat from public welfare. This politics is being implemented by the New Democrats in the USA and by the resurgent social democrats of Europe. Social democracy has from this point of view embraced economic neo-liberalism, though that does not mean it is simply the same as the new right. Rather, what is emerging is a distinctively centre-left version of a neo-liberal politics. One account of this process, which suggests the emergence of an international discourse as part of it, is that being developed by Pierre Bourdieu and his associates. Here is my translation of a description by Lois Wacquant of the international spread of the new 'penal state':

> We have to reconstruct link by link the long chain of institutions, agents and supporting discourses (advisory notes, committee reports, visits by officials, parliamentary exchanges, specialist seminars, academic and popular books, press conferences, newspaper articles, television reports, etc.) through which the new penal common sense (incubated in the USA), which is directed at criminalising deprivation and thereby normalising insecurity in employment, is becoming international.[15]

The international spread of a penal discourse (including such expressions as 'zero tolerance', used initially in the USA, then in Britain, then in other European countries) is part of the process. New 'tough' ways of dealing with youth crime or people sleeping rough in public places or begging are sustained and supported by this new penal discourse. Bourdieu and Wacquant refer more generally to 'a new planetary vulgate' which includes 'fetishised' terms such as 'globalisation', 'flexibility', 'multiculturalism', 'communitarianism', as well as more specific terms such as 'zero tolerance'.[16] The proliferation of political 'think-tanks' is relevant here – they have contributed 'new thinking' to the political field which contributes to spreading the international discourse of neo-liberalism.

It is not only governments that are incorporated within this new international order and discourse, it is also various other types of business and community organisations, and, importantly, the powerful international agencies such as the World Bank, the International Monetary Fund, and the Organisation for Economic Cooperation and Development. For instance, the World Bank published a policy research report on the 'old-age crisis' in 1994.[17] The 'old-age crisis' is the perception that demographic and social change mean that public welfare systems cannot provide adequately for the old without detracting from economic growth. The proposed solution is a combination of three systems:

1   A publicly managed system with mandatory participation and the limited goal of reducing poverty among the old.
2   A privately managed mandatory savings system.
3   A voluntary savings system.

The study concludes that 'a combination of different income security policies is more effective than any single approach and ... all countries should begin planning for their ageing populations now'. This combination of a reduced state provision focused on the poor, greatly expanded private pensions for those who can afford them, and an emphasis on personal saving is the basis for New Labour's pension reforms in Britain, but also for reforms being initiated in many other countries. The contraction of the social state is becoming an internationally harmonised process.

Part of international harmonisation of policy is the emergence of an international political discourse. Let me refer, as an example, to a discussion paper by the President of the World Bank published on the Internet in January 1999.[18] The paper is concerned with the development of a comprehensive, integrated and long-term approach to development and the alleviation of poverty, bringing together different international agencies (the International Monetary Fund, the World Trade Organisation, the World Bank itself, etc.) with national governments, the private sector, and civil society. The paper actually sets out a comprehensive framework for aspects of development which are the particular concern of the World Bank – 'the structural, social and human aspects'. What I want to focus on, however, is its view of what is now increasingly referred to as 'governance'. One striking similarity to New Labour is the focus on civil society and the use of the originally academic term 'civil society' in governmental discourse (rather common in the language of New Labour):

> In all its forms, civil society is probably the largest single factor in development ... by engaging civil society in projects and programs, better results are achieved both with design and implementation and usually greater effectiveness ... we all recognize more and more that local ownership is the key to success and project effectiveness.

The view of governance centres upon 'partnership' or 'cooperation' between 'participant groups' (including 'civil society'), and on the 'transparency' and 'accountability' of their activities – for instance: 'Such development should, in our judgement, be a participatory process, as transparent and as accountable as possible.' All of these words are part of New Labour's vocabulary of governance, and 'partnership' is one of the New Labour keywords.

A new language of governance appears to be emerging on an international basis and transcending boundaries between governmental and other types of organisation. An example of how this language of governance is being taken up by business comes from the contribution of a representative of a major international mining company at a seminar organised within the Economic and Social Research Council's project on global environmental change. According to a summary of the discussion in the seminar, the company representative referred to their 'experience in engaging with stakeholders as part of its global operations', and to a project with the World Bank on the formation of 'trisector partnerships' between industry, the World Bank, and 'civil society' for handling industrial development.

Difference and contestation in the field of political discourse

I referred in the Introduction to interviews with the Deputy Prime Minister John Prescott in January 1999 which included a focus on differences of language within New Labour. Prescott's interviewer on Radio 4 referred to these differences as follows:

> The point though is that the way that people in government talk about these things is important, you'd acknowledge that. Indeed it was Mr Mandelson's credo that the way you talked about things, the way you used language was very important, because it sent out messages. And you don't need to be told that a lot of Labour MPs – when they saw what you were saying, the language you were using, 'traditional values' albeit 'in a modern setting' – were saying: 'Look, here at last is a little more of the stuff we want to hear. He doesn't talk about "The Project" doesn't talk about "New Labour", he talks about "Labour".'

Such differences within New Labour are framed by differences within and around the Labour Party as a whole. Not everyone within the Labour Party is New Labour, and a number of important Labour Party figures are now outside the Labour Party, in many cases as a result of the dominance of New Labour. These divisions within the left and the centre-left can be seen, as I suggested in the introduction to this chapter, as a manifestation of the different effects New Labour's mitigated neo-liberalism has on different sections of the population, and they are constituted as differences in political discourse.

I have taken the following example from a book[19] written by two long-standing members of the Labour Party, Ken Coates (who is a member of the European Parliament) and Michael Barratt Brown. (They are now operating within the Independent Labour Network.) They are writing here about New Labour's view of what they call 'capitalist globalisation' ('the new global economy' in New Labour terms):

> Capital has always been global, moving internationally from bases in the developed industrial countries. What has changed is not that capital is more mobile ... but that the national bases are less important as markets and production centres. In other words, the big transnational companies are not only bigger but more free standing ... the European Union, far from offering a lead and a challenge to the nation-states of Europe, reinforces their status as clients of the transnational companies. Indeed, this clientism applies

not only to companies based in Europe ... While it is true that a national capitalism is no longer possible in a globalised economy, it is not true that national governments – and by extension the European Union – are totally lacking in powers to employ against the arbitrary actions of transnational capital. There is much that governments can do in bargaining – in making or withholding tax concessions for example ... But such bargaining has to have an international dimension or the transnational companies can simply continue to divide and conquer ... New Labour appears to have abandoned what remained of Labour's internationalist traditions ... Yet the ICFTU, the European TUC and the Geneva trade groups all offer potential allies for strengthening the response of British labour to international capital.

One notable difference between this extract and the discourse of New Labour is that 'transnational companies' are referred to as dominant actors in the global economy. In New Labour discourse, as I pointed out in chapter 1, they are elided. Their presence in this other Labour discourse helps to make the point that part of the character of the political discourse of New Labour is relational – its relationship to other political discourses which coexist with it in the same political field. That is what makes certain absences from the discourse of New Labour (such as the transnational companies) 'significant absences' or pointed absences, part of a covert dialogue with other discourses, a covert process (which may also on occasions become overt) of taking a distance from others.

What is also striking in this extract is the relationship of equivalence between 'transnational companies' and 'transnational' or 'international capital' (later also 'global capitalism'). Moreover, national governments (and the European Union) are represented as in a potentially antagonistic relationship to them ('employing powers against' them and acting in 'response' to them). This is a characteristic of certain left political discourses – 'capital' is to be contested, fought against. National governments are represented moreover as acting in alliance with trade union organisations (as well as non-governmental organisations more generally – see below) on an international basis in accordance with 'internationalist' traditions. 'Internationalism' here maintains its sense of the solidarity of labour, whereas in the discourse of New Labour it has come to refer to 'cooperation' between nation-states in the 'international community' (e.g. in bombing Yugoslavia). Notice also the concept of 'clientism', set up against 'employing powers against' or 'bargaining' with capital, which has no part in the political discourse of New Labour.

In discussing non-governmental organisations as 'essential allies for parties of the left to encourage and unite with in developing radical internationalist programmes in response to global capitalism', Coates and Barratt Brown write:

> Some NGOs ... have developed in their international rela-
> tions what professor Diane Elson, the Manchester
> economist, has called 'the economy of trust'. Most commer-
> cial organisations spend much time and energy on
> controlling, monitoring, checking and counter-checking
> their business transactions. In a highly competitive market
> they simply do not trust their suppliers or customers not to
> take advantage of them. There is an alternative – to build up
> a relationship of trust ... one of the lessons learnt by some
> NGOs working in the Third World, where for long there
> was a relationship of domination and exploitation [was that]
> nothing less than total openness and respect could build up a
> new relationship ... if all the words in New Labour's
> pronouncements about partnership and social markets,
> cooperation and not confrontation were to be taken seri-
> ously, the economy of trust would surely have a special
> appeal. Instead we find that 'the enterprise of the market and
> the rigour of competition' are always put before 'partnership
> and cooperation'.[20]

Part of the dialogue and polemic across different political discourses may be a critique of the other's discourse – though char-acteristically it is not New Labour in its position of dominance in the field that engages in such critiques (its dialoguing tends to remain implicit), but rather its more marginal opponents. In this case there is a critique of what New Labour says about 'partnership' and 'coopera-tion'. This is partly contesting the meanings given to these words within the discourse of New Labour, setting up a different discourse in which 'partnership' and 'cooperation' are articulated with 'trust', 'openness', and 'respect'. And it is partly claiming (in an apparent allusion to New Labour's favoured 'not only but also' relations, e.g. 'cooperation as well as competition') that there is a covert hierarchy in New Labour discourse, for example: 'enterprise' and 'competition' always come before 'partnership' and 'cooperation'. Recall my discussion in chapter 1 of how such relations and other lists cover over hierarchy and asymmetry.

There are other political discourses within the spectrum of the left and centre-left, some of them more marginal than the example above. Under the heading 'A Dud Deal', the Scottish anarchist publication 'Counter Information'[21] writes as follows of the Government's 'New Deal':

> Labour are restructuring the welfare system to benefit the bosses to an extent the Tories could only dream about. The New Deal attacks the entire working class. Resistance is vital.
>
> Under 25s unemployed for over 6 months are forced to attend the 'Gateway' interviews. They aim to find/pressurise 40% into an unsubsidised job.
>
> All others will be forced into [a number of alternatives are specified].
>
> Claimants who won't participate, or leave early, face having their Job Seeker's Allowance benefit cut completely for 2 weeks (4 weeks for a 2nd 'offence').
>
> The details for over 24s unemployed for over 2 years (starts in June), single parents, and disabled are not yet clear. Compulsion is probable for the unemployed. Labour deny compulsion will hit single parents, but increasing harassment is likely.

The key social actors in this representation of welfare are the Government (notice that it is simply 'Labour', not 'New Labour'), 'claimants', and 'the bosses', a vernacular way of referring to employers which is used in some sections of the left but never by New Labour. Nor indeed is 'the working class'. A metaphor of warfare is used ('attack', 'resistance'), and Government actions are represented as a form of violence ('compulsion', 'harassment', people being 'forced' or 'pressurised' into things). The penal language of New Labour is ironically referred to by the word 'offence' being used in 'scare quotes'.

Change in the political discourse of New Labour

In this section I am concerned both with how the political discourse of New Labour has changed over time, and with how that political discourse is actively constituted in documents, speeches, interviews, and so forth.

Let me begin with some points about the development of the political language of New Labour. The transformation of Labour into New Labour did not take place overnight, and it began well before Tony Blair became leader of the Labour Party. The 'modernisation' of the party was already underway while Neil Kinnock and John Smith were leaders. The Commission on Social Justice was set up by John Smith after the 1992 election defeat to consider in particular the relationship between social justice and economic efficiency. The 'Third Way' theme of 'economic efficiency as well as social justice', which claims that hitherto irreconcilable demands can be reconciled, is central to the Commission's report,[22] as is the language of 'social exclusion'. The report sets up what Levitas[23] describes as one of a number of 'false antitheses' between policies aimed at redistributing wealth and policies aimed at creating wealth.

The language of New Labour has been in formation since the beginning of the 1990s, and its development manifests an ongoing dialogue with the language of Thatcherism, in part an appropriation of it and in part an attempt to go beyond it (see the section on New Labour and Thatcherism above). Phillips[24] shows for instance how the Thatcherite thematisation of 'value for money' and 'waste' within public services were taken into the language of the Labour Party from the early 1990s (e.g. in a speech by Neil Kinnock in 1991: 'Value for money: that's what you get when you stop wasting £18 million of taxpayers' money a day propping up the Poll Tax'). She also quotes Tony Blair as shadow employment spokesperson in 1990 using a collocation which was subsequently to become a prominent element in the language of New Labour – 'rights and responsibilities' ('These are the issues of the new agenda. Rights and responsibilities, justice within the law, not injustice outside it.')

In a series of speeches at the beginning of 1996 Tony Blair elaborated the idea of 'stakeholding'. For a time, 'stakeholding' was seen to be the 'big idea' which provided a link between different parts of the emerging political position of New Labour – specifically between its commitment to 'enterprise' and strengthening Britain's competitiveness, and its commitment to social justice and community. However, it ran into difficulties. It proved to be a difficult concept to pin down, and was interpreted in many different ways, including ways which evoked forms of ('old Labour') corporate arrangement between government, business, and labour (trade unions) from which the Government were eager to distance themselves. The term had virtually dropped out of use before the general election in 1997, though according to Gould[25] 'the language of stakeholding may have withered, but the new approach underpinning it has prospered'. 'Stakeholding' is an interesting case for my purposes in this section of the chapter, first because it is a graphic illustration of how a political discourse can undergo quite major transformations over time, but second because it illustrates rather well the process of building and elaborating political discourse.

The texts of Blair's speeches at this time were so to speak doing political work – they were working the new vocabulary of 'stakeholding' together with other existing vocabularies, they were weaving new and existing vocabularies together into a new web. The result of this work is a new product – a new political discourse which is in many ways recognisably the same as previous New Labour discourse, but nevertheless also significantly different. Politicians and political analysts see particular speeches as landmarks or watersheds, and often refer to them. What gives a speech this special status is the quality of the political work it does. There are two aspects to the quality of the political work of a speech: intellectual and rhetorical. One question concerns the intellectual quality of a speech, the quality of the political position it articulates, its contribution to constructing a political discourse. Another question is about its rhetorical power, its capacity to enthuse and mobilise people, to capture their imaginations. Great political speeches do both – they put a coherent political vision in an enthralling way.[26]

Blair gave a speech in Singapore on the 'stakeholder economy' in January 1996[27] which may not have been a great speech, but was a good speech, and was seen as a watershed – as intellectually significant in launching 'stakeholding' as the big, integrating idea for which New Labour had been searching. I shall come to the Singapore speech shortly. Actually, some other speeches on the same theme around the same time were perhaps more rhetorically powerful – for instance here is part of a speech given in Derby on 18 January 1996:

> The stakeholder economy is the key to preparing our people and business for vast economic and technological change. It is not about giving power to corporations or unions or interest groups. It is about giving power to *you*, the individual. It is about giving you the chances that help you to get on and so help Britain to get on too: a job, a skill, a home, an opportunity – a stake in the success we all want for Britain. We will fight for that stake, working with you, in

partnership. The Tories fight only for the privileged few. We stand for the majority, the many.[28]

The audience for the Singapore speech was the Singapore business community, whereas this speech was addressed to a local British audience. Of course, most speeches by Blair reach much larger audiences through the media and are designed with that in mind; nevertheless their immediate audience also affects the way they are written. The extract from the Derby speech seems to be more fully worked rhetorically, more carefully designed to win a British audience to the new political vision. It works together a surprising number of important New Labour political themes in a short space (stakeholding, the link between greater equality of opportunity and Britain's economic success, partnership, the many not the few), putting a complex argument in a simple and accessible way.

Let me list some features of the extract which contribute to its rhetorical power. It is made up of quite a lot of simple sentences, which are effective in breaking up the message into easily digestible parts, and which are set off from and related to each other in a clear and pointed way. These include clear antitheses between what stakeholding is and is not (the second and third sentences – not 'giving power to the corporations' etc., but 'giving power to you' etc.) and between Tory and New Labour concerns (the last two sentences – 'the privileged few' versus 'the many'). The specialist and, for most people, unfamiliar term 'stakeholder' is reworded as an expression which is used in everyday language, '[having] a stake in' is glossed in everyday terms as 'chances that help you get on', and made concrete through specific examples – 'a job, a skill, an opportunity'. The complex link between equalising opportunity and economic success for Britain is made through metaphorically extending the everyday language of individual success to Britain – you 'getting on' leads to Britain 'getting on'. The idea of government enabling people to act rather than acting for them is worded first in an everyday way ('working with you'), then reworded as the key New Labour term 'partnership'. The audience is addressed directly ('you'), and the speech uses 'we' both exclusively (just for New Labour) to set up a 'we'–'you' relationship, and inclusively ('we all') in the 'one-nation' way.

Rhetorical work cannot ultimately be separated from intellectual work because any public elaboration of a political discourse is also working to persuade people. A great deal of preliminary talking and thinking goes on behind the scenes – Gould[29] provides a fascinating account of this. But as soon as political discourse goes public, it is rhetorically constructed, part of a political performance. The distinction between conceptual and rhetorical work is fine as an analytical distinction as long as we do not lose sight of their intimate relationship in practice.

Having said that, I want to focus on the intellectual work of the Singapore speech, the building of a new political discourse through weaving different themes and vocabularies together. For this we need rather a long extract from the speech:[30]

> I want Britain to be one of the really dynamic economies of   *1*
> the twenty-first century. ... We must ... make ourselves
> world leaders again.
>
> The key words are 'investment', 'quality' and 'trust'. The
> reason for investment is to create long-term strength. ... we   *5*
> must be moving up continually to higher-value-added prod-
> ucts. That comes through quality. ... The creation of an
> economy where we are inventing and producing goods and
> services of quality needs the engagement of the whole country.
> It must be a matter of national purpose and national pride.   *10*
>
> We need to build a relationship of trust not just within a
> firm but within a society. By trust, I mean the recognition of
> a mutual purpose for which we work together and in which
> we all benefit. It is a stakeholder economy, in which oppor-
> tunity is available to all, advancement is through merit, and   *15*
> from which no group or class is set apart or excluded. This is
> the economic justification for social cohesion, for a fair and
> strong society – a traditional commitment of left-of-centre
> politics but one with relevance today, if it is applied anew to
> the modern world.   *20*
>
> ... There is a real risk that, in this era of change, some
> prosper but many are left behind, their ambitions laid waste.
>
> We need a country in which we acknowledge an obliga-
> tion collectively to ensure that each citizen gets a stake in it.
> One-nation politics is not some expression of sentiment, or   *25*
> even of justifiable concern for the less well off. It is an active
> politics – the bringing of the country together, a sharing of
> the possibility of power, wealth and opportunity. The old
> means of achieving that on the left was through redistribution
> in the tax and benefit regime. But in a global economy the   *30*
> old ways won't do. Of course a fair tax system is right. But
> really a life on benefit – dependent on the state – is not what

most people want. They want independence, dignity, self-improvement, a chance to earn and get on. The problems of
35   low-pay and unemployment must be tackled at source.

The economics of the centre and centre-left today should be geared to the creation of the stakeholder economy which involves all our people, not a privileged few, or even a better-off 30 or 40 or 50 per cent. If we fail in that, we waste talent, squander potential wealth-creating ability, and
40   deny the basis of trust upon which a cohesive society – one nation – is built. If people feel they have no stake in a society, they feel little responsibility towards it and little inclination to work for its success.

The implications of creating a stakeholder economy are
45   profound. They mean a commitment by government to tackle long-term and structural unemployment. ...

The stakeholder society has a stakeholder welfare system. ... it holds the commitment of the whole population, rich and poor. This requires that everyone has a stake. The alter-
50   native is a residual welfare system just for the poor. After the Second World War, the route to this sort of commitment was seen simply as cash benefits ... But today's demands and changed lifestyles require a more active conception of welfare, based on services as well as cash, child care as well as
55   child benefit, training as well as unemployment benefit.

... we must build the right relationship of trust between business and government ... we need neither old-style dirigisme nor rampant laissez-faire. There are key objectives which business and government can agree and work
60   together to achieve. This 'enabling' role of government is crucial to long-term stability and growth.

The same relationship of trust and partnership applies within a firm. Successful companies invest, treat their employees fairly, and value them as a resource not just of
65   production but of creative innovation. ... We cannot by legislation guarantee that a company will behave in a way conducive to trust and long-term commitment, but it is surely time to assess how we shift the emphasis in corporate ethos from the company being a mere vehicle for the capital
70   market – to be traded, bought and sold as a commodity – towards a vision of the company as a community or partnership in which each employee has a stake, and where the company's responsibilities are more clearly delineated.

Let's begin with the sentence in which 'stakeholder' first appears (beginning in the 14th line of the extract): 'It is a stakeholder economy, in which opportunity is available to all, advancement is through merit, and from which no group or class is set apart or excluded.' The sentence weaves 'stakeholding' together with three other established themes in New Labour discourse – equality of opportunity, meritocracy, and social exclusion. It works the new theme into a new articulation with the established themes, which constitutes a new version of the political discourse of New Labour. It does so through setting up equivalences between words and phrases – 'stakeholder', 'opportunity is available to all', 'advancement is through merit', and 'no group or class is set apart or excluded'. What makes them equivalent is a common grammatical relation to *economy*: economy is a noun of which they are all modifiers. The three phrases also constitute a list. The preceding sentence sets up an equivalence between 'trust' and 'the recognition of a mutual purpose for which we work and in which we all benefit' in a different way – through explicit definition ('By trust, I *mean* the recognition of a mutual purpose', my italics.) The two sentences are linked by the pronoun 'It' which refers back to 'the recognition of a mutual purpose', and sets it up as equivalent to 'a stakeholder economy'. So a complex chain of equivalences, which works the new term 'stakeholder' into an articulation with a set of familiar ones, is built up in these sentences.

This is essentially what the conceptual work of political language comes down to: working different vocabularies (and, in more general terms, different languages) together into new articulations, and thus producing new articulations of political themes, i.e. new political discourses. But equivalence is only one relationship into which words and expressions are worked. There is also antithesis.* The next full paragraph (beginning in line 23) includes a combination of the two. First, an equivalence is set up across the first two sentences between 'an obligation collectively to ensure that each citizen gets a stake' and 'one-nation politics' through an implicit assumption – the second sentence only makes sense if we assume they are equivalent. In the third sentence, 'It' refers back to 'one-nation politics', which is set up as equivalent through the equative verb 'is' with 'an active politics' and then through a list with 'the bringing of the country together' and 'a sharing of the possibility of power, wealth and opportunity' (note that 'power', 'wealth' and 'opportunity' constitute their own embedded equivalence). So, once again, 'stakeholding' is articulated with established themes (especially 'one-nation politics').

The second and third sentences also set up an antithesis through the move from a negative verb ('is not') to a positive verb ('is'), between 'some expression of sentiment, or even of justifiable concern for the less well off' and 'an active politics' – implying the former is not 'active'. Presumably 'passive'? But the main antithesis is later in the paragraph. An equivalence is set up between 'redistribution in the tax and benefit regime', 'the old ways', 'a life on benefit', and 'dependent on the state'. Notice that these are contentious and persuasive equivalences – not everyone would accept that redistribution is 'old', nor that it entails 'a life on benefit', or being 'dependent'. The latter evokes controversial new right theories of welfare as causing 'dependency'. An antithesis is then set up between this chain of equivalences and another in the list: 'independence', 'dignity', 'self-improvement', and 'a chance to earn and get on'. These equivalences and antitheses in the latter part of the paragraph are not new. On the contrary, they are an established and relatively stable element in New Labour discourse. What is new is that 'stakeholding' is being woven into them.

I shall comment on equivalences and antitheses in the rest of the extract in a more selective and summary way. In the paragraph beginning in line 36 an equivalence is set up between stakeholding and 'which involves all our people'. There is an antithesis between success in establishing a stakeholder economy and failure. The latter being represented in negative terms through equivalences between 'waste talent', 'squandering potential wealth-creating ability', and 'deny the basis of trust', and between 'have no stake', 'feel little responsibility', and 'little inclination to work for its [society's] success'. Equivalences between the corresponding positive terms are implied (having a stake, feeling responsibility, feeling inclined to work for the success of the society). Notice particularly the implied equivalence between stakeholding and the important New Labour theme of responsibility.

With regard to a 'stakeholder welfare system', an equivalence is set up between stakeholding and 'the commitment of the whole population'. An antithesis is set up between a 'stakeholder' and a 'residual' welfare system – this can be seen as a reworking of a more familiar contrast between 'residual' and 'universal' welfare systems. Another antithesis, which we came across earlier, is between 'active' and (by implication) 'passive' conceptions of welfare. A series of equivalences is set up between 'active' and 'not only but also' relations ('services as well as cash', 'child care as well as child benefit', 'training as well as unemployment benefit').

The final paragraph (from line 62) deals with the stakeholder company rather than the individual stakeholder which is the main focus of the speech. These are the two main forms of stakeholding in New Labour discourse according to Driver and Martell.[31] A chain of equivalences is set up in the paragraph between 'trust', 'partnership', 'long-term commitment', 'invest', 'treat their employees fairly', 'value them [employees] as a resource not just of production but of creative innovation', and 'each employee has a stake'. And an antithesis is set up between this chain of equivalences and 'the company being a mere vehicle for the capital market'.

The cumulative and overall effect of these interconnected equivalences and antitheses is to work 'stakeholding' into an evolving web or network of political themes. Although equivalences and antitheses are important relations within that web, they are not the only ones. What they have in common is symmetry: if x is equivalent to y, then y is also equivalent to x; if x is in antithesis with y, y is also in contrast with x. But there are also asymmetrical relations. Actually, a few of the examples I have identified as equivalences are, on closer inspection, asymmetrical. For instance, the relationship between 'feel they have no stake in a society' and 'feel little responsibility towards it' in the sentence: 'If people feel they have no stake in a society, they feel little responsibility towards it and little inclination to work for its success.' We can call this asymmetrical relationship 'entailment' – feeling you have no stake entails feeling little responsibility, but feeling little responsibility does not entail feeling you have no stake.

The relation of entailment makes the connection between webs or networks of political themes and, what I called in the first chapter, the 'logic' of New Labour's political discourse. In this speech Blair develops that logic. The extract above incorporates an argument: if Britain is to be competitive, it has to be in the quality market, which requires the engagement of the whole country, as 'one nation'; but that depends on everyone having a stake in the economy. If they don't, then we lose both potential wealth-creating ability and the relationship of trust on which a 'one-nation' society is built. In terms of this argument, 'having a stake' or 'stakeholding' is what links together the two great themes of New Labour, its Thatcherite legacy, and its communitarianism: making Britain competitive and making Britain a cohesive, 'one-nation' society. Or in different terms: 'enterprise' and 'community' (which is the route to 'fairness' and 'social justice'). But the argument is built upon relations of entailment between major New Labour themes: being competitive entails entering the quality market (or: the knowledge-based economy);

entering the quality market entails the whole country working together ('one nation'); being 'one nation' entails everyone having a stake in the economy.

We can generalise from this link between argument and entailment by connecting it to the link discussed above between rhetoric and discourse. There are two interconnected processes simultaneously going on in the speech. On the rhetorical side, there is the process of argument – Blair is trying to persuade people by constructing a convincing argument in the course of the speech. On the discourse side, there is the process of classification, which includes the three relations discussed above (equivalence, contrast, and entailment). Any political speech is simultaneously working intellectually on the classification of political themes, and therefore on the political discourse, and working rhetorically on the political argumentation. There will be continuity as well as change in both – a speech may to a greater or lesser degree reproduce established classification and argumentation at the same time as being innovative in both.

The extract above comes from one of a series of speeches on the theme of 'stakeholding' which Tony Blair gave early in 1996. These speeches can be seen as exploratory attempts to extend the theme of 'stakeholding' across various areas of New Labour policy, attempts to work 'stakeholding' into an intellectually coherent and rhetorically convincing web with other New Labour themes – an exploration of its potential as a 'big idea'. The Singapore speech on the 'stakeholder economy' was followed by speeches dealing with the 'stakeholder society' and 'stakeholder politics'. The former included a new working of the relationship between 'stakeholding' and the theme of 'rights and responsibilities': 'We accept our duty as a society to give each person a stake in its future. And in return each person accepts responsibility to respond, to work to improve themselves.'[32] The latter included a new working of the relationship between the themes of 'stakeholding', trust, and devolution: a 'stakeholder democracy', 'trusting people to make their own decisions', 'devolving power outwards to the people'.

By contrast, a speech given by Blair to the South African Parliament in January 1999[33] made no reference to the theme of 'stakeholding', but there is a different attempt at a 'big idea' through working a new relationship between the theme of 'rights and responsibilities' and other themes. What is particularly striking is the working of the theme of 'rights and responsibilities' into the field of international relations, for instance:

The developed world has a responsibility to transfer resources, expertise and assistance to the developing world. The developing world has a right to expect this but also a responsibility to ensure that resources are used productively and for the benefit of the poor, not on misguided policies, white-elephant projects or even worse, the cancer of corruption.

The same language of 'rights and responsibilities' is applied here to international relations as to 'civic society' and the welfare state.

Summing up, the political discourse of New Labour is a process rather than a finished product, and we can see it in process by looking carefully at the language. But it is not an even process. It is not a matter of a single person (e.g. Tony Blair) or for that matter a team working single-mindedly on developing and elaborating the discourse. It is rather a process that involves a number of people who may be pulling in more or less different directions. It is a process that is cut through by different concerns, different occasions, and different circumstances. For instance, a central location of the process is in Tony Blair's speeches, yet they deal with many diverse issues, are addressed to many diverse audiences, and give many different inflections to the process.

I have referred to the ongoing search for 'the big idea'. The 'big idea' which has been prominent, if not always dominant, through the history of the Labour Party was replacing capitalism with socialism or at least changing capitalism in fairly radical ways to force it to respond better to the needs of working class people. New Labour arguably does not have a 'big idea' in anything like that sense – a cynical view is that it puts a lot of energy into trying to make the 'Third Way' look like a 'big idea', which it isn't.

Finally, it is important to appreciate that the process of constituting a political discourse is to some extent at the mercy of events. To what extent politicians and governments control events is contentious, but they are certainly always having to react to events they could not have foreseen, and thus develop their political positions and political discourse on territory they would not have chosen.

Conclusion

My concern in this chapter has been with process – with how the discourse of New Labour is continuously constituted in shifting relations with other discourses within and beyond the political field, which it draws upon, informs, contests, and so forth. This chapter concludes the discussion of the political discourse of the 'Third Way' which began in chapter 1. In the next two chapters I move on to my other major concerns in the book – first, the rhetorical style of the leader of New Labour, Tony Blair; and, second, the language of government under New Labour.

4

THE RHETORICAL STYLE
OF TONY BLAIR

As contemporary politics has become increasingly centred in the media, the prominence of leaders in the political process has increased. Political parties and governments are now more strongly identified in terms of the individuals who lead them than ever before – Thatcher and Blair in Britain, Reagan and Clinton in the USA. This public visibility can certainly give a misleading impression of what goes on in politics and government. Nevertheless, no political analysis can ignore the political identity and personality of the leader; and identity and personality centrally involve language, rhetorical style.

Politics is a social practice which sets up a range of positions for people involved. Party leader and, in government (depending on the political system), Prime Minister or President are such positions. Much of what particular politicians do and much of the way they behave follows from the positions they occupy. Having said that, there is considerable variation in how people perform in these positions. Indeed, it is these differences in performance that are decisive for political success or failure – parties do not need leaders who perform the role in a textbook fashion, they need leaders who perform the role distinctively, and are perceived to be distinctively better than others. People perform differently as political leaders depending upon their social identity (their social class, the cultural or regional community from which they come, their gender, etc.), but also depending upon their particular life history and experience. It is thus partly a matter of the social identity and personality they bring to the leadership position, but it is also partly a matter these days of how their attributes are honed and inflected on the advice of the political communications industry.

Political identity is constructed, built. Here is one of Blair's key advisers, Philip Gould, writing about a memorandum he wrote in 1994 called 'Consolidating the Blair Identity':

First I spelled out the strengths and weaknesses of Blair's position. His strengths were 'freshness and a sense of change; confidence and self-assurance; that Tony Blair is a new kind of politician; that Blair changes what it means to be Labour'. His weaknesses were that he could be perceived as 'over-smooth', 'too soft and not tough enough', and 'inexperienced'. In response to this, 'Tony Blair should not be what he is not. This will not work and will be counter-productive. He should not try to avoid the problem of youth by behaving with excessive gravitas. Nor try to avoid looking soft by behaving with excessive aggression. What he must do is build on his strengths, and build an identity as a politician that is of a piece with the political positions he adopts. He must be a complete, coherent politician who always rings true.'[1]

Gould writes in rather general and indeed vague terms, but he is partly alluding to Blair's language and rhetorical style, envisaging a process of development and construction certainly, but one that 'builds on' what is already there rather than attempting incompatible add-ons (such as an aggressive communicative style) which will prevent him 'ringing true'. Notice also that he envisages a process of 'building', which seeks coherence between political identity and political positions, a point I return to below.

A rhetorical style is not an invariable way of using language; it is rather a mixture of different ways of using language, a distinctive repertoire. Tony Blair does not always speak in the same way, but he has a distinctive repertoire of ways of speaking which he moves between in a recognisable way. Part of the variability of his style is to do with the variability of the genres within which he operates. For example, a political speech at a Labour Party conference or in Parliament entails a different use of language from that of a radio phone-in programme, television interview, Fabian Society pamphlet, or an article in the *Daily Mail*. Even within any one of these genres – let us say a political speech – Blair uses language in different ways to do different things, for instance to spell out Government policy, or to argue a contentious issue, or to establish a rapport and intimacy with his immediate audience.

My approach to Tony Blair's style in this chapter will be to show how he moves through different ways of using language, focusing on two examples in different genres: his speech at the 1997 Labour Party conference, and an interview he did in January 1999 on the BBC1 television programme 'Breakfast with Frost'.[2]

The speech was given at the first Labour Party conference after New Labour won power. The conference slogan was 'New Labour, New Britain', and Blair summarised his objective in the speech as follows: 'Today I want to set out an ambitious course for this country: to be nothing less than the model 21st century nation, a beacon to the world.' The interview was framed within the crisis of late 1998 and early 1999, which I referred to in the Introduction. It begins with questioning about ministerial resignations (especially Peter Mandelson's), as well as a scandal involving the Foreign Secretary Robin Cook, then it takes on the character of a broad review of major aspects of policy. I shall also discuss more briefly his style as a 'wartime leader' during the NATO attacks on Yugoslavia. This will allow me to say something about another important aspect of the variability of Blair's style – how it is changing over time.

Blair's rhetorical style is not purely a matter of language. It is a matter of his total bodily performance, of which what he says is just a part. It is a matter of how he sounds, how he looks, the shifting expressions on his face, the way he moves his head and other parts of his body. While it is highly important to try to capture this total bodily performance, it is very elusive, difficult to describe, and particularly difficult to describe in print. Ideally, we (author and readers) should be watching and discussing a video together, if not Blair in person.

Blair the 'normal person'

Leader identity in contemporary politics is generally built upon a tension between the public office and the private individual, the extraordinary position of the leader and the 'ordinary' person who holds it. In terms of language, this means a tension between the public language of politics and everyday language. Politicians differ not in whether they show this tension – they virtually all do – but in the particular forms it takes. According to his political biographer, 'a central component of Blair's appeal in the two years before he became leader was that he was recognisably a human being, that he did not sound like a politician … an impression he sought to reinforce when he became leader'.[3] Blair himself wrote:

> I feel like a perfectly normal person. I look at politicians who are older than me and I wonder when was the last time

they had their own thoughts to themselves in their own way without feeling they had to programme their thoughts to get across a message ... I don't actually feel much like a politician.

With the passage of time, Blair has come to be seen increasingly as a politician like others, and there is a certain irony about the way he dismisses programming 'their thoughts to get across a message' in the light of New Labour's preoccupation with being 'on message', as well as Blair's reliance on focus group research in determining how to move politically. Nevertheless, the tension between the 'normal person' and the politician remains, in a form which is an important part of Blair's style and of his apparent continuing popularity (at least according to opinion polls).

The sort of 'normal person' that Blair comes across as is crucial in defining his leadership style, and to his popularity. Gould's list of strengths is worth taking seriously. 'Freshness and a sense of change': Blair belongs to a different generation from that of previous political leaders, and he is an extremely young leader – he became Prime Minister just before his 44th birthday. In both respects he is strikingly similar to Bill Clinton, who is just seven years older than he is. Both belong to the generation that grew up in the 1960s and early 1970s, and both are (in Gould's words) 'a new kind of politician'. Part of that generation's experience is a discomfort with traditional forms of publicness, including traditional forms of political charisma and rhetoric – be it in the mould of Churchill or of the previous Labour leader, Michael Foot – and a corresponding preference for forms of publicness which are personally open and reveal people's 'normality' rather than disguising it behind a public facade. These new forms of publicness transcend social domains: for instance, there is a striking similarity between the style of Blair and the style of the prominent and successful British businessman, Richard Branson. An interesting question (for another book) is what links there are between leadership styles, discourses (see chapters 1–3), and genres of governance (see chapter 5) across different domains of contemporary social life, such as government and business.

In my view, Blair's political identity is anchored in his personal identity; or, more accurately, in how his personal identity is constructed in his public performances. Whatever public abilities and qualities he has built up – including, for instance, a capacity to be 'tough' which Gould saw as lacking in 1994 – it is a crucial part of his political identity (and his apparent continuing popularity) that the 'normal person' regularly emerges from the public figure. He rarely fails to 'touch base', so to speak. What this means in terms of language and the overall 'bodily performance' that constitutes Blair's rhetorical style is that Blair's political performances are inflected by the language and communicative style of Blair 'the normal person'. In this section I will trace some of the forms which that inflection takes.

So what is 'base'? What sort of 'normal person' does Blair come across as? Not only relatively young, but youthful. When he suddenly grins in the course of a political interview, the impression is of irrepressible youthful vitality and enthusiasm, and, as Gould notes, 'confidence and self-assurance': Blair comes across as a relaxed, firmly anchored and well-adjusted personality in a generally rather sordid political world. I should add that he comes across as middle class – more specifically, northern middle class as shown by certain details of the accent he shifts into at these more personal moments. We are virtually all cynical about politics these days but, for many, the repeated evidence of an engaging 'normal person' with an infectious smile redeems Blair's unavoidable political manoeuvring. This is likely to wear thin eventually and is already perhaps doing so – cartoonists and satirists (such as the television satirist Rory Bremner) are already getting the measure of Mr Blair. But my impression at the time of writing is that it still has considerable potency. Let me emphasise that what is at issue is a public construction of normalness: we should not assume that Blair in his private life is necessarily the 'normal person' he seems to be in public. Inevitably, there are parts of his private personality that will be different from what we see in public.

An interview is more like a conversation than a political speech, more interactive, more dialogical, and therefore a genre in which the 'normal person' is more likely to be prominent. But there are parts of the interview in which Blair speaks in a public, authoritative and essentially monological way conventionally associated with politics. Here is one example, where Blair is responding to a question about the European Union and its new currency, the euro:

> and it is as I said in the e:m Wall Street Journal it is essential
> for our country not to end up walking away from Europe or
> believing there is any future at all in being on the sidelines
> in key debates in Europe there's no future in that for Britain
> . and even though I know I've got a large part of the media
> against me on this and even though I know I've got a lot to
> do in convincing the country on this it would be the biggest

failure of leadership imaginable if I failed to point out to the British people the consequences . of walking away from Europe and leaving ourselves without influence in it Europe matters to Britain and in or out of the euro we have got to be positive constructive engaged shaping the debate about Europe's future

Part of the authoritativeness is in the language and specifically in the modality,★ the degree of assertiveness. Blair makes a number of categorical, authoritative assertions (e.g. 'it is essential … not to end up walking away', 'there's no future in that for Britain', 'it would be the biggest failure of leadership imaginable'); but part of that authoritativeness is also in the way he says it. Three of the assertions are delivered in a slow, emphatic way in which he stresses each word separately ('it is essential for our country not to end up walking away from Europe', 'it would be the biggest failure of leadership imaginable', 'Europe matters to Britain'). Each assertion is accompanied with sharp emphatic vertical movements of the head and/or hand. Slowing down and using body language in this way is how Blair makes important points in his political speeches too.

But even here the 'normal person' is not entirely absent. There is a shift towards speaking in the first person singular in the middle of this extract ('even though I know I've got a large part of the media against me on this and even though I know I've got a lot to do in convincing the country on this'). What is also important and characteristic here is Blair's capacity to stand back from and comment upon the position he is in, the difficulties he faces – the 'normal person' reflecting on the politician. Furthermore, certain details of Blair's accent vary according to whether he is speaking more publicly or more personally, and one of them is the pronunciation of 'I': either rhyming with 'eye' (more public) or with an 'a' sound (more personal – a part of his northern middle-class accent). 'I' is pronounced in the latter way twice in this extract – in 'I said' and the second time Blair says 'I know'. Otherwise it is pronounced in the former way. This may seem trivial, but such minor details are important in conveying the message that even when Blair is being most public and political, the anchorage in the 'normal person' is still there.

The interview continues as follows:

FROST: and how do you deal with that problem of that problem which you rightly mentioned of the of the way some of the strongest elements of the press are ranged against this policy on

Europe I mean . the Murdoch press e:m the Telegraph Group the Mail Group I mean right there you have a huge preponderance e:m how does that affect your policy making or does it just affect your policy presentation or does it just affect the fact that you don't read those papers?

BLAIR: [*laughs*] no it means that you've got to go over their heads to a large extent . and and reach the people . and let's have an honest debate . about the euro I mean before Christmas we had some of the most ludicrous stories about what Europe was planning to do with our taxes and our lifestyle and all the rest of it there is a big big question . about Britain's future . and the future direction of the country and . I believe that Britain cannot stand apart from Europe Britain has got to be part of Europe I believe that . as I say the test on the euro is that it has to be . in our national economic interest . but what we cannot do . is stand aside as a matter of principle

In this extract there is a more marked movement between the public and the personal. First of all, Blair responds to Frost's joke at the end of the question with the sort of engaging grin (as well as a laugh) I referred to above, strongly conveying a sense of the 'normal person'. This is sustained in what he goes on to say. The pronoun 'you', used in a non-specific way (where 'you've got to' is an informal equivalent of 'one has to'), belongs to everyday language, and Blair's use of it brings the perspective of everyday life into government. Other politicians do similar things, but what makes Blair's style distinctive is a whole set of features – some of which taken singly are not at all distinctive to him. Blair also pronounces 'got to' in a conversational way with the 't' sound replaced by a glottal stop (a feature of what has recently been referred to as 'Estuary English', a fashionable style of pronunciation based upon cockney).

The part with the most sustained conversational style is: 'I mean before Christmas we had some of the most ludicrous stories about what Europe was planning to do with our taxes and our lifestyle and all the rest of it'. Blair uses 'I mean' (as well as 'you know') frequently in his more conversational talk. This is a feature of his style, which has been widely noticed and picked up by satirists. Its presence here marks the shift of style. 'Ludicrous' is a conversational word rather than a political one, and 'all the rest of it' is a conversational way of saying 'and so forth' or 'etcetera'. At the same time, both the delivery and the body language shift to being conversational – for instance, Blair expresses his contempt by elongating the first syllable of 'ludicrous', and his head movement, instead of being vertical as it was earlier, is a rather idiosyncratic oscillation from side to side. From 'there is a big big question . about Britain's future', the style shifts back – to authoritative assertions underlined by shifts in the pace and rhythm of delivery and emphatic vertical head and hand movements.

Summing up on this example, it shows first of all that Blair has developed the capacity to speak with authority, he has acquired the public, political language to do so; yet he has retained the capacity to portray himself as a politician who is redeemed by an engaging normalness – a capacity which shows itself communicatively in the inflection of the political language with a personal language.

Frost raises the issue of the peace process in Northern Ireland – the search for a political settlement of the differences between Republicans and Unionists:

FROST: Northern Ireland. Today is it on schedule?

BLAIR: – yes I think it is e:m . e: I mean partly because of the e: the strikes in the in the Gulf e:m there was an overshadowing of of the huge breakthrough before Christmas in the agreement of the e: cross-border bodies e:m and also the agreement of the the new departments in the Northern Ireland assembly . we literally have this . thi– this one last . part . e:m of the jigsaw to put in place now e: which is getting the new executive set up and dealing with the issues like decommissioning which are a problem in respect of it . but e:m I mean I jus– I can't believe we've come this far. to go back now . I mean if you think back eighteen months people would never have believed we could have come this far in Northern Ireland . you've got a whole . new situation there and I just hope there exists the imagination and vision on all sides to to bring it to fruition

Blair's response is not the conventional, bland, reassuring political response. He gives the impression of being open and honest (whether he is or not is of course another matter), and that impression depends on a rather substantial presence here of the language of the 'normal person'. He begins by cocking his head on one side in a gesture which indicates that he is thinking before he replies – there is quite a long pause – and when he does reply the intonation (his voices rises rather than falls on the word 'is') indicates only a qualified judgement that the peace process is on schedule. Notice that there are three instances of 'I mean', a favoured feature of Blair's conversational style as I indicated above. The hesitations ('e:m', 'e:') and repetitions ('of of', 'the the', 'this . thi– this') are further conversational features which are markers of a person responding in a thoughtful way rather than a politician reeling off prepared answers. When Blair says 'thi– this one last . part . e:m of the jigsaw to put in place now', he opens his hands and looks down at them (as he says 'part') as if physically trying to grasp the missing part, and then smiles broadly at Frost. Shortly afterwards he shifts to speaking in the first person: 'I mean I jus– I can't believe we've come this far. to go back now'. What comes across is a genuine, heartfelt conviction which is conveyed by the body language as well as the language – he vigorously shakes his head and smiles slightly as he says 'I mean I jus–', and 'can't believe' is delivered with heavy stress on both words and a downward movement of the head. At the end of the extract he expresses hope that the necessary vision and imagination exist. Overall, Blair gives the impression of being deeply committed to the peace process and optimistic about it, but open about its uncertainties – a frankness and degree of personal involvement which has been unusual in politics and which again is an effect of the communicative presence of the 'normal person'.

A political speech is a rather more difficult environment for the 'normal person' to emerge from than an interview; nevertheless, the anchoring of Blair the politician in Blair the 'normal person' also applies in speeches. In the early days of his leadership, Blair seemed ready to bring personal emotion into politics, and to challenge in so doing the line between the personal and political. His speech on the death of Princess Diana in the autumn of 1997[4] was rather a good example. As I said in my comments on part of the speech in the Introduction, he combines an everyday emotional language ('utterly devastated', 'in a state of shock') with formal, ceremonial expressions of regret ('we are today a nation in mourning') in a way which brings his own emotional reaction as a 'normal person' (as he puts it, 'like everyone else') into his official task as Prime Minister. That occasion was of course an exceptional one, but Blair does sometimes bring personal emotion into more conventional political contexts.

He begins the conference speech for instance as follows:

> thank you very much I– . perhaps I should just quit whilst I'm ahead [*laughs*] e:m [*audience laughter*] . thank you for that wonderful welcome – – well. it's been a very long time waiting for this moment . and all I can tell you . is that I am deeply . proud. and privileged . to stand before you . as the new . Labour prime minister of this country [*applause*]

Before Blair speaks, he stands on the platform acknowledging the applause with a rather embarrassed smile on his face. He begins speaking quietly, in a low-key way. First of all he makes a joke with a nervous little laugh, using the vernacular expression 'quit whilst I'm ahead' as a way of claiming his 'normalness' (though using 'whilst' rather than 'while' makes it sound middle class). An indication of his emotional response to the occasion is that his voice breaks slightly when he says 'wonderful'. There is then a long pause (about four seconds) during which he is looking down at his notes as if to ready and calm himself. He then speaks slowly and quietly, and stands with a serious expression on his face which suggests he is fighting to control his emotion while the audience applaud – the emotional character of the moment is also expressed in their faces.

But it is mainly through humour that the 'normal person' is brought into the speech, as in the following example:

> we won . because we are New Labour . because we had the courage to change ourselves and the discipline . to take hard decisions while remaining united . the lessons we learnt in opposition we carry on applying in government the moment we stop is the moment we will stop being in government [*applause*] and I say to you even now . in fact especially now . no complacency . I mean I know I'm slightly obsessive about this thing [*laughter*] and I perhaps went over the top when . I phoned Millbank Tower on election night to complain that people were behaving as if it was in the bag look I was told . so far we've got 150 seats the Tories have got 6 it's quite hard to persuade the media this thing's on a knife-edge [*laughter*] but . but . however still no complacency . because the first of May was the beginning not the end . we have never won two full consecutive terms of office never and that is one more record I want us to break [*applause*]

There is a change of style in the middle of this extract, beginning from 'I mean I know I'm slightly obsessive', and shifting back with the repeated 'but . but'. Blair is telling a joke, but a joke at his own expense, based upon insider knowledge about his obsession with 'complacency'. As I have already noted, in his more conversational style Blair frequently prefaces statements (as in this case) with 'I mean' – the frequency with which he uses it is a part of his distinctive style – and in this case, 'I mean' is a marker of the shift in style.

So too are the slight accent changes I have already referred to – 'I' is pronounced with an 'a' sound ('a know') and 'look' loses its final consonant (it is replaced by a 'glottal stop' – another feature of 'Estuary English'). 'Over the top' and 'in the bag' are elements of vernacular vocabulary, but again very clearly of middle-class vernacular. The conversational style is also marked by understatement ('slightly obsessive', 'perhaps went over the top', 'quite hard'). At the same time there are changes in Blair's 'body language' – from a serious facial expression with a characteristically firmly closed mouth conveying resoluteness to a smile; from vertical movements of head and hand to underscore the serious message of 'the moment we stop is the moment we will stop being in government' to a slow rotation of the head from left to right and back again, which allows him to scan the whole audience (another Blair characteristic). There is also a shift in the pace of delivery – from a slow deliberate spelling out of the serious message to a much quicker conversational pace of talking. These shifts into a more vernacular, everyday style are also shifts into a more interactive style – Blair is engaging with the audience. Judging from the very favourable reaction they receive from the audience, they seem to be important for the effectiveness of Blair's style (though I am using a video recording of the speech, which is itself a professionally produced piece of Labour Party publicity, so audience reactions are likely to be carefully edited).

Getting tough

I have already referred to Blair's authoritative style in the interview – the style he uses for 'giving the line' so to speak, setting out his position or that of the Government. This style is more prominent in political speeches, but it uses similar resources:

> no cockiness either about the Tories not even now . they're not dead . they're just sleeping . but let their fate serve rather as a warning to us . what the people give the people can take away . we are the servants they are the masters now [*applause*] last year . we were talking about what we would do . this year . we're doing it . that ten-point contract with the British people . we are honouring it . we said we would get more money into schools and hospitals we have . two point two billion pounds more than the Tories planned to spend next year . we said we would sign the Social Chapter and we did we said we would retire trade union rates at

GCHQ on May 19 free and independent trade unions came
back to GCHQ [*applause*]

There is a series of injunctions directed to the party ('no complacency', 'no cockiness') and authoritative statements (e.g. 'we won .
because we are New Labour', 'what the people give the people can
take away', 'we said we would get more money into schools and
hospitals we have'). The first part is Blair 'giving the line' to the party,
the second is Blair speaking for the party to the wider audience.

The authoritativeness of this style is again partly marked in the
language and partly in the 'body language'. As regards the language,
there are, apart from the three injunctions, a large number of mainly
concisely worded statements. They are categorical, authoritative statements. In other styles, including other parts of the interview, Blair
modalises his statements with expressions like 'I think'. If he had said
in this case 'I think we won because we are New Labour', or 'I think
the Tories are just sleeping', he would sound considerably less authoritative – his authoritative statements would be transformed into
opinions. Some of the categorical statements are given a special
salience through being slowed down: for instance, 'two point two
billion pounds more than the Tories planned to spend next year'.
Slow deliveries are often followed by applause, as in the case of 'on
May 19 free and independent trade unions came back to GCHQ',
and in fact they seem to be used by Blair to elicit applause. The body
language is equally categorical, as I have already indicated above – the
modality is bodily as well as linguistic. Blair's facial expression is
serious. Statements (especially those slowly delivered) are accompanied by emphatic vertical movements of head and hand, and the
more salient ones are terminated with a firmly set mouth which
makes Blair look rather grim.

There is a particular use of this authoritative style which is a
central part of New Labour and of Blair's style – 'getting tough'. I
pointed earlier to the significance of Blair's slogan 'tough on crime,
tough on the causes of crime' in moving New Labour to the centre
and winning middle-class support. 'Tough' is a New Labour keyword,
and being 'tough' is a basic part of Blair's political identity. However,
as Gould pointed out,[5] Blair began with a disadvantage in this regard
because 'he could be perceived as ... "too soft and not tough
enough"'. He has had to learn to be 'tough', and the 'resolute'
Margaret Thatcher has been a model and inspiration here, as well as
Bill Clinton (who also affects the combination of being 'tough' and
being 'fair'). From Gould's account, it seems that the value of the

word 'tough' in a populist appeal to 'middle England' was established through focus group research – this seems to be a case where New Labour's language has been directly shaped by focus groups.

Here is an example of Blair being 'tough' in the speech:

> but here's the hard choices. the money will be there . but in return . we modernize the system . no failure . no muddling through . no second best . high standards the pursuit of excellence discipline and leadership support from home not for some children . in some schools . but for all children in all schools [*applause*] each school that needs it . and every educational authority will be set targets for improvement . failing schools and educational authorities will be taken over . teacher training will be reformed . head teachers will have a proper qualification and poor teachers will go no people [*applause*] and I'll say why . people say my job is pressurized . so is teaching . and don't let anybody think we are tough on bad teaching because we don't value teachers . we are tough on bad teachers precisely because we do value good teachers who need high quality teachers working alongside them [*applause*] and parents have to play their part . there will be home–school contracts for all pupils. I say sign them . there will be new measures to tackle truancy and disruptive children new homework requirements support them . and when a school disciplines a child . why not back the teacher [*applause*] . the high ideal of the best schools in the world . reached through hard choices

Before he begins speaking, Blair wags his finger at the audience in a school-masterly way. The first section of the extract consists of short parts separated by pauses. At the end of each, Blair's mouth is set into a tight-lipped expression, which repeatedly conveys in a bodily way the message of 'toughness'. Notice the simple present-tense form of the verb in 'we modernize the system' – not 'we will modernize' or 'we intend to modernize', which would both mitigate the message that this is definitely going to happen. From 'no failure' to 'for all children in all schools' there is a list of phrases without verbs. These are apparently to be interpreted as negative injunctions (e.g. 'there must be no failure') and positive injunctions (e.g. 'there must be high standards'). I shall come to the question of why they are formulated in this implicit way below. The next section, from 'each school that needs it' to 'poor teachers will go' is again divided into relatively short parts separated by pauses, and again each ends with Blair's tight-lipped, 'resolute' expression. The 'toughness' is also there, as is the modality, in the repeated modal verb 'will' (just as 'modernize' is firmer than 'will modernize', so 'teacher training will be reformed' is firmer than, for instance, 'we intend to reform teacher training'). Blair's hand movements are also significant – including sharp downwards movements of his right hand with a single finger extended, actually tapping the table with his finger as he says 'need high quality teachers working alongside them'. The authoritarian language is also applied to parents: obligations are explicitly imposed upon them with the modal verb 'have to', there 'will be' home–school contracts rather than, for instance, 'parents will be invited to undertake' such contracts, and parents are directly asked to 'sign', 'support' and 'back' – the first two are imperative verbs (though the force of the first is mitigated by 'I say').

A consensus politician

There is a significant absence in Blair's style both in his political speeches and in his interviews – an absence of polemic. I briefly referred to it in comparing New Labour with Thatcherism in chapter 3, and in fact the point is perhaps best made by a comparison between Blair and Thatcher. Thatcher's style is highly polemical and oriented to combating enemies. Here, for instance, is Thatcher speaking about trade unions:[6]

> If some unions continue to act as an engine of inflation, and a drag on improvements in industrial efficiency, they will go on alienating themselves from the people, including those whom they represent. ... It is a patent contradiction for [them] to urge the Government to treat pensioners more generously, when it is the inflation which they have helped to create that diminishes the value of the pensioners' money. To claim social conscience in these circumstances can fairly be described as humbug.

Blair seems to avoid such polemic where possible. Inevitably, there are circumstances in which the Government does take a position against particular groups of people, and Blair can be 'tough' in such cases, as we have just seen, but he tends not to polemicise against them, but rather to seek consensus around the need to be tough. Blair might have been 'tough' in the above extract through polemicising against those whose failings he is alluding to – teachers, head teachers, educational authorities, parents. But characteristically he doesn't do that. He avoids confrontation in various ways while still being 'tough'. The failings he alludes to are alluded to through nominalisations which do not identify explicitly who failed ('failure', 'muddling through', 'second best') – hence the list of phrases without verbs I referred to above, rather than formulating the injunctions explicitly. Ways of acting in response to failure are formulated as passives ('will be set targets', 'will be taken over') so that the interventions of Government are backgrounded. The most contentious Government action, sacking 'poor teachers', is referred to intransitively ('poor teachers will go') as if the teachers would leave of their own accord. The focus is generally on the positive, action to overcome failings, rather than the failings themselves. Blair thus manages to be 'tough' and authoritarian towards particular social groups – be it 'poor teachers', those 'dependent' on welfare, or criminals – without explicitly demonising them. The myth of 'one nation' is sustained while treating certain of its parts in sometimes draconian ways.

The contrast between the styles of Thatcher and Blair carries over into interviews. Thatcher was notorious for her combative interview style, interrupting interviewers, rejecting their attempts to change the topic, challenging their questions, and so forth. Blair by contrast tends to be a model of politeness in his political interviews, listening attentively to questions, being careful not to start speaking before the question is complete, giving ground to interviewers when they interrupt him. Here is one small example from the 'Breakfast with Frost' interview where Frost asks a question ('what about you?') while Blair is talking, and Blair compliantly shifts from whatever he was about to say next to answer the question:

BLAIR: and again let's just be honest about this if you look at parts of the Liberal Democrats they're modern social democrats . I mean the– . you know the– there's there's lots in common
FROST: what about you?
BLAIR: well I think the– if I was to sit down and say the ideological differences between myself and some of the . Liberal Democrats they're pretty small

Avoidance of polemic is an important feature of Blair's political style. It accords with the New Labour commitment to 'one-nation' politics oriented to building consensus around policies, which are represented in a value-neutral way as 'modernisation'. In that sense it meets Gould's recommendation that Blair's identity as a politician should be 'of a piece with the political positions he adopts'. It also accords with an intolerance of dissent within the ranks of the Labour Party, and a focus on promotion and the management of consent when it comes to public consultation on policy, rather than debate and dialogue. And, perhaps most insidiously, it accords with the claim that the 'new politics' of the 'Third Way' transcends 'old' divisions between left and right – effectively a claim to go beyond politics. New Labour has some strongly authoritarian tendencies that are somewhat mitigated and disguised by the search for consensus, which is manifested in these features of Blair's style.

There is of course no guarantee that Blair's consensual style will not change. During the NATO bombing of Yugoslavia he made a number of sharp polemical attacks on Milosevic, and at the time of writing (July 1999) there are indications that this style could be applied within domestic politics. Blair angered public sector workers and unions by making what was widely seen as a direct attack on the former:

> One of the things I would like to do, as well as stimulating more entrepreneurship in the private sector, is to get a bit of it in the public sector as well. People in the public sector are more rooted in the concept that 'if it's always been done this way, it must always be done this way' than any group I have ever come across.

He went on to say that he bore 'scars on my back' after two years of trying to force change in the public sector. These comments were reported as 'unscripted', and they evidence again Blair's 'personalness' and humour, so they are far from the severe polemic of war. Nevertheless, they were seen as a new stage in the campaign to 'modernise' the public sector, a move into direct attack, which was made doubly offensive by the fact that they were delivered to a City of London audience of venture capitalists. They provoked what was widely interpreted as a rebuke from Blair's deputy John Prescott.

The conviction politician

Blair often formulates policies of the Party and the Government in a personal way as if it were simply a matter of his own commitments and aspirations. An example from the speech:

it's pretty simple you know the type of country that I want .
it's a country . where our children . are proud and happy to
grow up in feeling good not just about themselves . but
about the community around them . I don't want them
living in a country . where some of them go to school
hungry . unable to learn because their parents can't afford to
feed them . where they can see drugs being traded at school
gates . where gangs of teenagers . hang around street corners
. doing nothing spitting and swearing abusing passers-by . I
don't want them brought up in that sort of country . I don't
want them brought up in a country where the only way
pensioners can get long-term care . is by selling their home .
where people who fought . to keep this country free . are
now faced every winter with the struggle for survival
skimping and saving cold and alone waiting for death to take
them [*applause*] and I will not rest . until that country is
gone . until all our children live in a Britain where no child
goes hungry the young are employed and the old are cher-
ished valued till the end of their days [*applause*]

The personal focus is sustained through this extract, beginning
with 'I want', then the three occurrences of 'I don't want', and finally
'I will not rest'. The values of the Party are transposed into the aspirations and commitment of the leader who comes across (in the
Thatcher vein) as a 'conviction politician'.

But there is more than speaking personally to being a 'conviction
politician'. One characteristic element of Blair's style, both in interviews and in political speeches, is that when he argues for a position,
often a contentious or disputed one, he often appears to do so with real
personal conviction. Again, the 'normal person' inflects the politician.
This style is in contrast with the more authoritative style identified
above – where Blair is setting out his own or the Government's established position rather than arguing a case. One rough-and-ready visual
indicator of a shift between the styles is whether or not his forehead is
furrowed – once he moves into arguing his forehead tends to become
more frequently and more deeply furrowed.

An example of his argumentative style is the following answer to
Frost's question on the sensitive issue of the relationship between the
Labour Government and the Liberal Democratic Party. Blair has
supported various forms of involvement of the Liberal Democrats in
government which have given rise to fears in his own party of a
coalition or even a merger:

FROST: What about the subject of the Liberal Democrats? e:m there was a story yesterday in one of the papers and other stories about the fact that three of your Cabinet are not . are not keen at all on e: getting close to the Liberal Democrats and on the idea of a e:m referendum on PR and so on. Do you plan to still proceed with that – near-marriage shall we say?

BLAIR: [*laughs*] well I'm still proceeding with the cooperation yes because it's it's right and it's in our interests to do so and again I . say to people just discount those type of stories. I mean this is something we've agreed ages ago . and I think it's sensible . if for example in areas like e:m . the constitution or indeed in respect of e:m education it may be or any of the issues which matter to the country you can work with another political party because there are lots of things we have in common with the Liberal Democrats why not do it? I mean what's the point of sitting there and saying we just have our own tribal positions and [*inhales and shakes his head, smiling*]

There is a shift in style from 'and I think it's sensible'. First of all there is a change in grammatical mood* – instead of making statements, Blair is now asking questions ('why not do so?', 'what's the point of sitting there …?'), more specifically, rhetorical questions whose answer is assumed in asking them. The formula used in the second question ('what's the point of …?') is very much a conversational one. But he is also speaking in a way that signals personal involvement and commitment. He stresses the word 'I' when he says 'I think that's sensible'. The pitch of his voice rises as if he was involved in a heated argument, and he also talks faster. He keeps glancing at Frost and then away from him until he asks the questions, when he keeps his eyes on Frost, simultaneously furrowing his brow and reaching his highest pitch. His face is serious and earnest until he reaches the questions, then he has a bemused slight smile, which turns into a full smile at Frost after each question. What is difficult to convey in a written description is the appearance of authenticity – Blair gives the impression (to this viewer at least) of bringing a real personal commitment to the political issue. An important aspect of it is 'common sense'. He significantly uses the word 'sensible', and the rhetorical questions, leaving the second question incomplete, and the bemused smile when asking the questions – all suggest that this is a matter of common sense, and that Blair is struggling from his commonsensical position to see what problems people could possibly have with 'cooperation'.

The following extract comes from the speech:

and I say to you . that the size of our victory imposes a very special responsibility on us . it is to be a government . of high ideals and hard choices. not popular for one time but remembered for all time not just a better government than the Tories but one of the great radical reforming governments of British history [*applause*] it is . to modernize Britain as we modernized the Labour Party . to build a Britain not for the few but for all the people . it will require change . hard choices . I know this country can make those hard choices . if we . show how . and why – this is a great people the British people . they don't fear change . look at our history we are one of the great innovative peoples . from the Magna Carta to the first Parliament to the industrial revolution . to an empire that covered the world . most of the great inventions of modern times . have Britain stamped on them . the telephone the television the computer penicillin the hovercraft radar . change . is in . the blood and bones of the British people . we are by our nature and tradition . innovators adventurers pioneers [section omitted] even today . in Britain . we lead the world in design pharmaceuticals financial services telecommunications . we have the world's first language English . Britain today . is an inspiring exciting place to be . and it can be much more . if we face the challenge . of a world around us today . that has has its finger on the fast-forward button . where every part of the picture of our life is changing changing constantly . so today I say to the British people . the chains of mediocrity have been broken . the tired days are behind us . we are free to excel once more . we are free to build that model twenty-first century nation to become that beacon to the world . creative . compassionate . confident of our place in that world . and you know when people say to me sorry that's too ambitious sorry it can't be done I say to them this is not a sorry country we are not a sorry people it can be done if we have the will and courage and determination to do it

One striking feature of this extract is the dialogue that is implied through stressing certain words in a way which suggests Blair is responding to things that had previously been said. This is the effect of stressing, 'is', 'are', and the modal verb 'will' ('Britain today *is* an inspiring exciting place to be', 'we *are* free to excel', 'we *are* free to build', 'it *will* require change' – I am using italic here to mark stress). Other cases are: 'if we *face* the challenge', 'the chains of mediocrity have been *broken*', 'the tired days are be*hind* us', which ascribe 'the challenge', 'the chains of mediocrity', 'the tired days' to other unspecified voices with which Blair is implicitly in dialogue. An argument is being conducted against unspecified others, and again Blair brings passion and conviction to the argument, marked in the language by the repeated references to his message ('I say to you', 'I say to the British people', 'I say to them'), and by the alternation between speaking for the people ('we') and speaking for himself ('I'). But the conviction and passion again are largely in the delivery and the body language – speaking within a relatively high pitch range, the appealing half smile on his face, his furrowed brow, hand movements such as bringing the two open hands together to symbolise unity, and so forth.

Blair's poetic

Part of Blair's form of conviction politics is the claim to be in tune with the people, a claim which Thatcher also made. In the following extract from the speech this edges into a visionary and poetic form:

> yes we are keeping our promises . but I want us to do more than keep our promises . I sense the British people demand more of us too . now people ask me . the highlight of the election . well it was . driving from home to Buckingham Palace that morning . along streets . we'd driven hundreds of times past soulless buildings and sallow faces on their way to work . this drive – was so different . as we turned into Gower Street people watching our journey on TV came pouring out of the doorways waving clapping shouting with an energy and excitement . that went beyond anything I imagined would happen . they were liberated . theirs were the smiles of tolerant broad-minded outward-looking compassionate people . and suddenly they learnt . that they were in the majority after all . as one w– woman put it to me . that morning . we've got our government back . and with them I could sense confidence returning to the British people compassion to the British soul unity to the British nation . and that all three . would give us new-found . strength . you see the people were yearning . for change in

their country at a time when they could see that we . had
had the guts . to modernize and change our party the two
came together and the result is a quiet revolution now
taking place and it is led by the real modernizers not me .
the British people they were the ones who had the guts to
do it

Blair is trying to capture and convey the mood, the atmosphere,
after the election, and the values which it expressed, and at the same
time he is constructing himself as sensitive to the mood, able to grasp
it and be in tune with it. There is something of a mythical narrative
here – the story of how the leader at the moment of assuming leadership enters into a mystical communion with the people. In trying
to convey the mood Blair is using language in an aesthetic, poetic
way – working the surface of the text, so to speak, to create a picture
in language, in the parallel structure (adjective + noun) and allitera-
tion ('s' and 'l' sounds) of 'soulless buildings and sallow faces', the
conjunction of verbs ('waving clapping shouting'), the metaphor of
'pouring', and the unusual sentence structure ('theirs were the smiles
…'). Again, Blair's delivery and body language also contribute to
evoking the mood – pausing dramatically after 'this drive', evoking
people's excitement in his own smiling and enthusiastic face, and
evoking their behaviour and the values it showed by giving prominence to each of the conjoined verbs and adjectives ('waving
clapping shouting', 'tolerant broad-minded outward-looking compassionate'), with the same pronounced downward pitch movement on
each word. The repeated verb 'sense' ('I sense the British people
demand …', 'I could sense confidence returning …') suggests the
leader's instinctive understanding of and rapport with the people.
And the leader interprets the people to the party ('you see the people
were yearning for change'), expressing through 'you see' his conviction that the privilege of interpreting belongs to him – 'you see' is a
vernacular expression used in explaining things to people in contexts
where there is a clear line between the one who knows and the one
who doesn't. I don't personally find this more poetic style of Blair's
convincing – it comes across to me as rather indifferent amateur
dramatics.

Blair the wartime leader

There is a certain irony in the fact that the leader who, according to
Gould, could be perceived as 'too soft and not tough enough' has

been widely perceived during NATO air attacks on Yugoslavia as the toughest and most resolute of NATO leaders. Here is an extract from a major speech on 'the doctrine of the international community' delivered during the Kosovo crisis:[7]

> This is a just war, based not on any territorial ambitions but on values. We cannot let the evil of ethnic cleansing stand. We must not rest until it is reversed. We have learned twice before in this century that appeasement does not work. If we let an evil dictator range unchallenged, we will have to spill infinitely more blood and treasure to stop him later ...
>
> We have five objectives: a verifiable cessation of all combat activities and killings; the withdrawl of Serb military and paramilitary forces from Kosovo; the deployment of an international military force, the return of all refugees and unimpeded access for humanitarian aid; and a political framework for Kosovo building on the Rambouillet accords. We will not negotiate on these aims. Milosevic must accept them ...
>
> Just as I believe there was no alternative to military action, now it has started I am convinced there is no alternative to continuing until we succeed. On its 50th birthday NATO must prevail. Milosevic had, I believe, convinced himself that the Alliance would crack. But I am certain that this weekend's Summit in Washington under President Clinton's leadership will make our unity and our absolute resolve clear for all to see. Success is the only exit strategy I am prepared to see.

The force of this language is partly a moral force and partly a political force – it is a combination of Blair being righteous and being tough. Both the ethnic cleansing in Kosovo and Milosevic himself are constructed in moral (and indeed religious) terms as 'evil'. 'We' (constructing NATO as a moral community) are under a moral obligation to reverse the former and challenge the latter (notice the strong modalities of 'we *cannot* let', 'we *must not* rest'). This is based in our 'values'. The war is morally legitimised as a 'just war'. So much for the righteousness. The toughness is also conveyed through strong modality ('we *will not* negotiate', 'Milosevic *must* accept', 'NATO *must* prevail'), and syntactically through the accumulation of concise and strongly modalised assertions (especially in the first paragraph). Notice that Blair speaks categorically both in the first person plural for NATO as a whole ('we will not negotiate') and in the first person singular for himself: 'success is the only exit strategy I am prepared to see'. Part of the toughness is constructing himself as personally committed in this way, as well as in the curt and ironic dismissal of speculation in the media and elsewhere about NATO's search for 'exit strategies'. Another significant feature of Blair's rhetorical style here is that he associates himself with a historical tradition of political leadership through adopting elements of a more formal and traditional political language, a language sharply set off from the everyday, a language which might have been used by Churchill or Thatcher and which therefore implicitly claims a continuity with such leaders. The moral categorisation of the Serbian side as 'evil' is part of this, as is the expression 'blood and treasure' as a way of referring to the human and financial costs of war, but also the verb 'prevail' in the sense of 'win', 'resolve', and even the verbs 'stand' and 'range'. (See chapter 6 for further discussion of this speech.)

Blair's qualities of leadership certainly seem to have been transformed by the war. He emerged, not only in Britain, but internationally as a 'strong' leader. This affected not only his language but also his visual appearance. I was particularly struck at the time by a feature in the German newspaper *Die Zeit* under the main headline 'A vision for the Balkans', and the sub-heading 'Even Serbia needs European help: a *Zeit* interview with Tony Blair about NATO strategy and the post-war period'. The fact that Blair's views are aggrandised into a 'vision' is one indication of his new stature. But the article also included what struck me as a new photographic image of Blair, a new, harder and stronger Blair.

Conclusion

I have focused in this chapter on different ways in which Blair uses language, and how he moves between them, how they are brought together in his speeches and interviews. A central theme has between the tension between the public figure, the politician, and the 'normal person' – the particular form which this tension takes in the case of Blair.

Recall Philip Gould's judgement that Blair is 'a new kind of politician'. Is there perhaps finally something enigmatic about Blair, something that is difficult to pin down, which constitutes his novelty as a politician, and which centres upon the relationship between the 'normal person' and the public figure? The way in which the public figure is always anchored in and, in a sense, redeemed by the 'normal person'? In so far as that is so, sustaining the power of the enigma depends upon a continuing sense of the authenticity of Blair the 'normal person', a continuing trust in Blair as a person. But that itself is difficult to sustain in the relentless exposure he is subject to in the media, not to speak of the attentions of satirists and cartoonists. What seemed to be his distinctive personality tends to be revealed as performance. It is partly a generational matter, the transposition into a new domain of a new mix of elements, a new style, which is commonplace elsewhere. Blair's generation (and the same is true of Clinton's, though British and American versions of the style are somewhat different) handles power differently, be it in business (for instance, Richard Branson), education, or politics. They are more laid-back, and rather than drawing a line between the public person and the normal person, they build upon the latter to constitute the former. It is a matter of a change in taste, a new aesthetic, a new mood. Perhaps Mr Blair after all is not that special.

Commentators will differ in how critical they are of Blair. His political persona is clearly a crafted one, based upon calculations of what will work, fed by focus group research. His constructed personality reassures those who are able to see themselves included within it – the white, middle-class, young, successful and confident. On the other hand, it implicitly excludes those who can't, including the substantial body of losers in this increasingly polarised society. Blair's political identity gainsays his claimed concern to 'tackle social exclusion' and achieve an inclusive society.[8] More harshly, this pretence, this extension of the marketing of commodities into the marketing of politicians, makes the claimed concern with values and morality look decidedly hollow. But is Blair really to blame for such distasteful features of contemporary public life? Does he have any alternative to going along with them? Perhaps not, but the question remains: Is the gap between what Blair claims to be and what he inevitably is consistent with his moral stance?

5

THE LANGUAGE OF GOVERNMENT

Writing in *The Economist* in September 1996,[1] Tony Blair said that 'the challenge facing us is to take a working constitution, respect its strengths, and adapt it to modern demands for clean and effective government while at the same time providing a greater democratic role for the people at large'. The reference to 'clean' government is a response to the accusations of 'sleaze', which dogged the Conservatives in their last years in government. What I want to focus upon is the relationship between making government more 'effective' and making government more democratic. Both are included in New Labour's aspiration to 'modernize' government in Britain. For Blair and his colleagues, they are compatible, they go together. But for others, there is a basic contradiction in the way New Labour has gone about 'modernizing' government since winning office in 1997. On the one hand, considerations of effectiveness have led to a substantial centralisation of power; on the other hand, the Government has initiated a whole series of major constitutional reforms and changes in government, which appear to constitute a substantial decentralisation of power.

There are various interpretations of this apparent paradox.[2] Some suggest that New Labour is trying to have it both ways and is avoiding the 'hard choices' which Blair is so fond of talking about. Or that the Government has simply failed to grasp the radical, decentralising consequences of its own constitutional reforms, especially the Scottish Parliament. But it is possible to see a coherent logic in New Labour's programme of 'modernization', a devolution and, in a sense, 'dispersal' of government[3] which entails a transformation but not an abandonment of close control from the centre. Whether New Labour can succeed in reconciling centralisation and decentralisation in this way is another matter. I shall begin this chapter by giving an account along these lines, drawing especially on Barnett.[4] I shall then discuss how a focus on language can contribute to understanding and analysis of New Labour's approach to government. I look at a particular case, the language of New Labour's welfare reform programme.

Corporate populism

It was the Conservative politician Lord Hailsham, referring to a Labour Government in the 1970s, who described the British form of Cabinet government as an 'elective dictatorship', but that description only really caught the popular imagination during the eighteen years of Conservative rule dominated by Thatcher. The Thatcher Governments were widely perceived as having undemocratically used the 'levers of power' to impose 'Thatcherism', despite the fact that they never had the support of the majority of voters and had virtually no support in certain areas of the country, especially in Scotland. This together with a sense that too much Conservative power for too long had led to corruption and 'sleaze' undermined public trust in government and led to widespread demands for reform, which New Labour incorporated in its 'modernisation' programme. In opposition, New Labour associated itself with the sort of programme for radical reform advocated by, for instance, Marquand and Hutton, including the idea of a 'stakeholder democracy', treating people as citizens in all domains of social life, and giving them a voice in decision-making, including for instance in the workplace.[5] In government, New Labour has retreated from its more radical commitments (for instance its proposed legislation on freedom of information).

Barnett[6] suggests that the clearest expression of New Labour's approach to 'modernizing' government is its introduction of an 'annual report'. Tony Blair in his introduction to the 1998 report wrote that 'Changing a government is like sweeping away the entire senior management of a company', and explained that the document was designed to help the public pass judgement on the Government because 'trust matters. In all walks of life people act as consumers not just citizens.'[7] New Labour's admiration of business corporations is widely documented, but according to Barnett the Government actually sees itself as a business corporation providing competitive services for its customers.

From this perspective, New Labour's commitment to devolution and to the 'dispersal' of government (giving greater involvement especially to business and voluntary organisations) is analogous with the dispersal of production amongst subsidiaries and contracted suppliers in modern business corporations. It does not imply an

abandonment or weakening of control from the centre, but a transformation in the nature of central control. Since entering
government, New Labour has both strengthened and transformed
the centre. The power of Downing Street, the Prime Minister's
private office, press office and policy unit, and of the Cabinet Office
has increased. Peter Mandelson was appointed as 'minister without
portfolio' inside the Cabinet Office to coordinate the work of
government departments, and a Strategy Committee of the Cabinet
was set up (the Prime Minister, the Deputy Prime Minister, the
Chancellor, the Foreign Secretary). At the same time, the Cabinet
itself barely meets, and the House of Commons is in Barnett's words
'treated with contempt'.

The main transformation in the nature of the power of the centre
is in the role of 'special advisers'. Special advisers are in an ambiguous
position between the political party and the Government – they are
political appointments, but are members of the civil service. By June
1998 the number of special advisers was almost double the number
in the Major Government (73 as compared with 38). Moreover, the
role of special advisers has changed. They are now no longer
predominantly policy experts (typically academics), but in the words
of the *Guardian* correspondent Hugo Young 'the minister's personal
familiars, whose prime talent, if any, lies in explaining what the
minister wants to get across: the guardians of access and the messen-
gers of perception'.[8] They are also commonly referred to as
'minders', pointing to their role in protecting 'their' ministers from
the outside world.

Control from the centre has shifted towards ensuring coordination, and controlling what Young refers to as 'perception'. The former
is illustrated by the prominence given to exemplars of what Blair
likes to call 'joined-up government' launched from the centre, such as
the Social Exclusion Unit which was set up to coordinate the work
of ministries in 'tackling' social exclusion (see chapter 2). Joined-up
government is problem-oriented, with the centre defining the problems and the broad strategies for 'tackling' them, closely monitoring
the performance of agencies in pursuing those strategies, and
controlling performance through a combination of inducements
('money for modernisation', as Gordon Brown puts it) and sanctions
(e.g. closing down 'failing' schools). The latter centres upon the
person of the Prime Minister's press secretary, Alistair Campbell. Not
only is Blair constantly shadowed and prompted by Campbell in both
his Government and Party public appearances, New Labour has also
changed the rules of procedure for Government ministers to require

all major interviews, media appearances, press releases, and speeches to be cleared first by Downing Street. Controlling the presentation and perception of policy is no longer a secondary matter, it is virtually inseparable from policy making, and advisers like Campbell seem now to be inside the process of policy making.

New Labour's preoccupation with discipline and control within the Labour Party is part of this logic, and the way it has extended even into the process of devolution is not an irrational contradiction but a predictable consequence of the overall logic. This has happened in Scotland through the rigorous vetting of Labour candidates for the Scottish Parliament in terms of their loyalty to New Labour, in Wales through what is widely perceived as London's imposition on a resistant Welsh Labour Party of Alan Michael as Labour leader in the Welsh Assembly, and in London through strenuous efforts to prevent the Labour MP Ken Livingstone standing for mayor. These are all clear indications that (whether Blair is the 'control freak' he is accused of being or not) devolution in no way entails New Labour relinquishing central control.

The accountability of this corporate form of government is seen in terms of its 'responsiveness' to public opinion, and it includes what Blair refers to as 'experiments in democracy' – for instance the setting up of a 5,000-strong 'people's panel' and constant dependence on 'focus groups' to tell the Government how its policies – and its language – are perceived. But being responsive to public opinion is only the passive side of an equation that also includes an active process of forming it. A media strategy is prepared for all significant Government initiatives – they are 'trailed' in the media before being properly launched, and there is a systematic 'follow-up'. This has been described as 'government by media spin'.[9]

But the Government sees its task as entailing more than influencing opinion. There is a telling statement in the Green Paper on welfare reform published in March 1998[10] (which I discuss in some detail below): 'Our ambition is nothing less than a change in culture among benefit claimants, employers and public servants – with rights and responsibilities on all sides' (section 3.6). New Labour is attracted, as I suggested in chapter 2, with respect to 'social exclusion' by the idea of government as 'changing culture',[11] changing the cultures of not only those in government but the public in general. Changing culture is centrally a matter of changing language – getting people to see their relationships in terms of rights matched by responsibilities depends upon getting people to accept and internalise that discourse – to talk and think about their relationships using the words/concepts 'rights', 'responsibilities', 'duties', and so forth. Changing cultures, and hence changing discourse, is made important within New Labour's governmental logic – it is essential if the centre is to take on the new role of coordinating and controlling perception. This is one important reason why it makes sense to analyse the politics of New Labour with a focus on language.

New Labour, as I have indicated in chapter 2, has been quite heavily influenced by Demos, a 'think-tank' which ironically was established by the former editor of the Communist Party journal, *Marxism Today*, Martin Jacques, together with Geoff Mulgan who now works in the Prime Minister's policy unit. Some of New Labour's thinking on the 'modernisation' of government seems to have come from Demos. But we might also get some insights into possible future developments in New Labour's modernisation strategy by looking at what Demos authors are saying about government. Perri 6 (the pseudonym under which the research director of Demos writes) has published a series of papers on modernising government (referred to in the last paragraph). In one of them for instance[12] s/he suggests that tomorrow's government will be based upon three principles: prevention (rather than 'cure'), integration ('joined-up government') and intervening to change cultures. Elements of this futuristic model are already evident in New Labour.

Interventions by the Government to change the people go beyond the sort of culture change to which I have referred to include the whole strategy for education and training. The New Labour Government is quite explicit about aiming to equip people to succeed within the 'new global economy'. Transforming them culturally is a part of that – for instance transforming attitudes to welfare and work so that people accept unstable working lives with little job security and an ongoing need to retrain and re-skill, and see welfare as doing no more than easing the transition back into work. What is not explicit here is the relationship of New Labour's governmental corporation to the real business corporations that dominate the 'new global economy'. This is the old question of the relationship of the state to particular interests, which arises no less sharply for New Labour than for its predecessors, despite its rhetoric of 'one nation' and 'inclusion'. In the contemporary context it is the question of how the nation-state functions within – and, according to some, services – the neo-liberal economy.

Looked at in terms of the emergent global structures of neo-liberalism and the role of nation-states within them, New Labour's 'modernisation' of government can be seen perhaps as a local instantiation of a new emergent 'complex' – using that term in the same way as it has been used in reference to a 'military-industrial complex' especially in the USA, a networking and convergence of interests and perspectives and strategies between industry and the military. The new 'complex' is based upon what in New Labour discourse are called 'partnerships' – between central government, the new national assemblies, local government, business, the 'third sector' of voluntary organisations, academic research and education, and so forth. These hitherto more autonomous domains are being drawn more tightly together into what is widely being called a form of 'governance' which transcends and makes partly redundant the old divisions between domains. 'Partnership' is a key concept and a key word. It is important however to distinguish this new 'networked' form of governance as a model and aspiration from the messier realities; whether such networks can be sustained in the face of diverse interests and agendas is an open question.

Language in New Labour's form of government

The central tension I have referred to above between the centralising and decentralising tendencies of New Labour is also a tension between two different modes of practice within government, administrative/managerial and political, which is partly a tension between two different ways of using language within government: promotional use of language and dialogical use of language. What I want to argue in this chapter is that, despite a discourse and rhetoric of government, which often represents the processes of government as political and dialogical, the processes are in fact overwhelmingly managerial and promotional. In subsequent sections I shall show in some detail the promotional and managerial nature of processes of government under New Labour, even when what is supposed to be going on is public consultation about proposed policies.

Spaces for dialogue have apparently been added to the processes of government by New Labour – the genres of government seem to have changed in this respect. After all, the widely used 'focus groups' are precisely spaces in which citizens can enter into dialogue about matters of policy. Moreover, Government web-sites now offer plenty of inter-active spaces where citizens can directly enter into dialogue with members of the Government. But none of these constitutes substantive dialogue. What is 'substantive dialogue'? I want to suggest that dialogue within the process of government is only substantive, only real as opposed to apparent dialogue, if it meets the following conditions:

1   People decide to come together, and can come back together.
2   Access is open to whichever sections of society want to join in –
    there is 'equality of opportunity' to join and to contribute.
3   People are free to disagree, and their differences are recognised.
4   There is space for consensus to be reached, and alliances to be
    formed, but no guarantees.
5   It is talk which makes a difference – it leads to action (e.g. policy
    change).

It is clear that the new forms of 'dialogue' appearing within the
governmental process of New Labour are problematic in terms of
these conditions. Take focus groups as an example. People do not
decide themselves to come together or come back together. They are
usually paid to come together by a communications consultant or
researcher. Access is determined by whoever organises the group.
There is space for disagreement and for consensus, but the notion of
alliances is meaningless – there is no continuity, nothing to bind these
people together beyond the given occasion. And whether the talk
makes any difference is entirely outside the hands of those involved.
Focus groups are not real dialogue in terms of these criteria, nor are
the interactive web-sites set up by the Government. First, because
they are not properly interactive (members of the Government do
not enter directly into exchanges with members of the public), and
second because it is entirely up to those who are supposedly silently
reading contributions whether the 'dialogue' has any effect on policy.

Is there not a mismatch with respect to government between
New Labour's self-representation and its action? According to Tony
Blair, writing before the general election, the programme of constitutional reform would aim 'to strengthen the rights and obligations of
citizens; to take decision-making closer to the people; and to improve
the democratic credentials of Westminster'.[13] And here is Blair
writing about 'Active Government: Partnership and Decentralisation'
in his 1998 pamphlet[14] on the 'Third Way':

> The democratic impulse needs to be strengthened by
> finding new ways to enable citizens to share in decision-
> making that affects them. For too long a false antithesis has
> been claimed between 'representative' and 'direct' democ-
> racy. The truth is that in a mature society representatives will
> make better decisions if they take full account of popular
> opinion and encourage public debate on the big decisions
> affecting people's lives. Across the West new democratic

experiments are under way, from elected mayors to citizens juries ... The demand for more democratic self governance is fed by better educated citizens and the free-flow of information provided by new technology and media. We must meet this demand by devolving power and making government more open and responsive. Devolution and local governance are not just important in themselves: open, vibrant, diverse democratic debate is a laboratory for ideas about how we should meet social needs.

There was an even more radical formulation in Blair's 'John Smith Memorial Lecture' in 1996: New Labour would aspire to 'a politics in which we are giving power back to the people ... a politics which treats people as full citizens, gives them greater power over government'.[15]

There is a characteristic mixture here of different formulations of the governmental process which range from what sounds like a programme for radical democracy ('giving power back to the people', 'democratic self-governance') to devolution ('devolving power') to involving people more in decision-making processes ('take decision-making closer to the people', 'enable citizens to share in decision-making') to making government more transparent and being more 'responsive' to public opinion. All of these are general and indeed vague formulations of reforms to be undertaken by the Government, and they all invite the question: How exactly do you propose to do that? Putting it differently, they are all open to interpretation, and 'the devil is in the detail'. The very fact of this mixture of the radical ('democratic self-governance') and the relatively tame ('making government more open and responsive') in the same breath, so to speak, might suggest that this is mere talk, discourse out of touch with action. But how to evaluate the relationship between words and action, the adequacy of words to action, whether action that is taken constitutes 'giving power back to the people' or not? The relationship between words and action is not a transparent relationship but a matter of contested interpretation, and an important part of politics is argument over whether words match actions and vice-versa (see chapter 6).

The New Labour discourse of government includes a positive evaluation of public dialogue and debate. Blair writes of 'encouraging public debate on the big decisions affecting people's lives', and more effusively asserts that 'open, vibrant, diverse democratic debate is a laboratory for ideas about how we should meet social needs'. More concretely, the Green Paper on welfare reform asserts that 'it is vital that reform is informed by full debate on the proposed framework. We are consulting widely on the contents of this Green Paper and we want your views', and Blair in his Foreword to the Green Paper writes that 'we want all the nation to be part of [the process of reform]. There will be consultation and time for discussion at every stage. Our objective is to build a genuine national consensus behind change.' I shall argue below that 'building a national consensus' in the case of welfare reform has in practice been seen by the Government in terms of managing consent through promoting its reform proposals rather than in terms of stimulating 'open, diverse, democratic debate'.

I think there is an important issue here which affects, but also transcends, the politics of New Labour. There is a great deal of talk about debate and dialogue in contemporary society, and an overwhelming consensus that the more debate and dialogue on matters of public concern, the better. At the same time, there is no clarity or consensus about what debate or dialogue mean. That is why it is important to raise the normative question I introduced above: What constitutes 'real' or 'substantive' dialogue or debate? One of the central problems of contemporary politics is the squeezing out of the 'public sphere', of spaces where people can openly dialogue over matters of common concern free from the constraints of both the state and the market, and in a way which can influence government.[16] Most of what now passes as public debate takes place in the mass media and especially the broadcast media, which means that it is constrained by market factors. The argument over what constitutes 'real' dialogue is a central part of the political struggle over the public sphere. (New Labour's record here is not too impressive. For instance, shortly before the general election, around 300 literacy specialists were invited to a discussion of New Labour's literacy policy. The 'discussion' took the form of a series of speeches from the platform which took up most of the day, followed by a short period for questions and comments from the invited specialists.)

Partnership

'Partnership' is a New Labour keyword. The following relatively early statement gives a sense of the wide range of 'partnerships' which New Labour sees as an essential part of its way of governing:[17]

we believe that there should be effective and fruitful partnership arrangements at all levels in the Party and between

127

> the Party and a future Labour Government. Beyond this …
> a future Labour Government should also seek to establish a
> wholly new partnership with the British people.

The document from which this is taken was an important strategy document, entitled 'Labour into Power' and significantly subtitled 'A Framework for Partnership', produced a few months before the 1997 general election.

The main collocations of 'partnership' in the New Labour corpus show a clear focusing of 'public–private' partnerships, partnerships between Government and business. The expression 'public–private partnership' (or closely similar ones such as 'partnership between the public and private sectors') occurs 19 times in a total of 126 instances of 'partnership', and 'partnership between Government and business', 'government in partnership with business' or similar expressions occur a total of 20 times. The other meaning of 'partnership' is inter-national relations (e.g. 'if Britain is to build a new partnership with China'). Collocations which occur infrequently include partnership 'between teachers and parents', 'between employers and employees', and 'between Government and the people'.

'Partnership' in practice seems often to be linked with a term which New Labour does not use as a descriptor of its own policies, though it did apply it in opposition to arguably similar Conservative policies – 'privatisation'. One contentious example is the so-called 'stakeholder pension', another is the Private Finance Initiative. A Green Paper on pension reform was published by the Government in December 1998 under the title 'A New Contract for Welfare: Partnership in Pensions'.[18] What many saw as a move towards privatisation of pension provision was constructed in the Green Paper as 'partnership': 'state and private provision working together in a partnership to ensure everyone can achieve an adequate income in retirement'. ('Together' is also a New Labour keyword, and a remark-able 43 out of the total 161 occurrences are in the collocation 'work together', with a further 25 occurrences in the related collocations 'bring together', 'come together', and 'achieve together'.) The 'stake-holder pension' is a private pension scheme for 'middle and higher income earners', with certain Government guarantees.

The Private Finance Initiative is another example of 'public–private partnership' which has been as contentious as private pensions. It is a way for public services to embark on capital spending programmes (e.g. building new hospitals and schools) without Government funding – the hospitals or schools are built by private businesses which then lease them to the public services over an agreed time period, at the end of which the private businesses are the owners. The advantage is public service development without increased public spending. Critics of the scheme argue that the major disadvantage is that public services will be forced into cutting their staff in order to meet the exorbitant costs of leasing back these facilities. Once again, the term 'partnership' seems to be giving a favourable gloss to a relationship which some would describe in more negative terms.

Media spin

For the rest of this chapter I shall focus upon a particular case, that of the New Labour welfare reform, and I shall be arguing in particular that the welfare reform process has been largely managed through managerial and promotional means rather than democratically through dialogue.

The Government's plans for welfare reform received an early setback in December 1997 when forty-seven Labour MPs voted against a Government proposal to cut the rate of child benefit for new claimant lone parents (a further 57 abstained). The Government's response was to prepare carefully the ground for the welfare reform Green Paper, a consultation document setting out the Government's overall strategy for welfare reform which appeared in March 1998,[19] and subsequent stages in the reform process. It was announced that the Prime Minister would take part in a 'welfare roadshow', touring the country to explain personally why welfare reform was necessary. His personal commitment and determination were foregrounded in media reporting of the plans for the 'roadshow' – Blair himself said in a television interview: 'I shall go out and fight for my position and say what I believe in.'

The 'welfare roadshow' is a good illustration of New Labour's management of news and 'media spin' (I am drawing on Jones' account[20]). The day before the 'roadshow' was launched with a speech by the Prime Minister in Dudley, his press secretary, Alistair Campbell, told the press lobby briefing that the Government believed it was vital for the debate to be based on 'facts and not fiction, myths or scare stories', and referred to a series of 'welfare reform focus files' just produced by the Department of Social Security setting out facts and figures about various benefits. He gave a foretaste of what Blair would say in Dudley, including the claim that 'benefit fraud was costing the country £4 billion a year, enough to build one hundred new hospitals'. Campbell added that although

the Prime Minister was ready to consult, no one should underesti-
mate 'his determination to see it through'. On the morning of the
Dudley speech Blair published articles in two national newspapers,
The Times and the *Mirror*, using virtually the same words as Campbell.
For instance, in the latter: 'Benefit fraud – estimated at £4 billion a
year – is enough to build one hundred new hospitals ... But no one
should under-estimate my determination to see this through.' The
campaign was carefully orchestrated both over a longer timescale
with the use of the 'focus files' and the 'roadshow' to prepare the
ground for the Green Paper, and over short periods such as the
careful and orchestrated trailing of Blair's speech in Campbell's press
statement and Blair's articles. The risk of unpredictable and uncon-
trollable media uptake of the speech is minimised by trailing the
speech in a way which presents it in the way the Government wants
it to be seen – which puts a particular 'spin' on it.

The importance of 'spin' is most obvious in the case of complex
documents or situations which might be presented in various ways,
and where Government control of perception is therefore crucial. An
example is the publication of the Welfare Reform Bill in February
1999.[21] I have already referred in chapter 1 to the article which Blair
wrote for the *Daily Mail* on the day the Bill was published, specifically with respect to its authoritarian language.[22] The headline of
Blair's article is: 'It really is the end of the something for nothing
days', and the article foregrounds 'a fundamental break with the past'
and 'a new ethic of rights and responsibilities' in terms of 'powerful
new signals to all benefit applicants' (which are actually set out as
bullet points in the article):

- If you can work, you should work.
- Those who are dishonest will not get benefits.
- If you can save, you have a duty to do so.
- If you are working hard to raise a family, the Government guar-
  antees that you will not be in poverty.
- If you are unable to work, you will get the security you need.

I discussed in chapter 1 the way in which 'toughness' is conveyed
both by the style of these 'signals', as well as the description of the
reforms as 'tough', and the photograph of the Prime Minister
looking exceptionally grim and severe. What this article does is put a
particular spin on a rather complex Bill – it manages the way it is
perceived, highlighting what the newspapers front-page headline calls
'the crackdown'.

Media 'spin' works through summaries. One characteristic of language in government is the constant production of summaries. For instance, many documents (the Green Paper on welfare reform, for example) begin with summaries of the whole document, maybe preceded with a foreword, which gives a different summary of the document, by a minister or the Prime Minister. The document will then be summarised again in press releases, in articles such as the one I am discussing here, in speeches, and in press reports like the *Daily Mail's*. Summaries are always from one perspective or another, they are always interpretative, and it is never enough simply to ask if they are 'accurate'. 'Spin' is just a particular function of summarising. It is also often through differences in summaries that political differences within the Government as well as between the Government and other parties or groups are played out.

In fact the 'spin' in this case is a double process, involving both the Prime Minister's own trailing of the Bill in the article, and the reports in this newspaper (as well as others) based upon both the article and press briefing. Part of the art of 'spin' is calculating what additional emphases and foregrounding newspapers like the *Daily Mail* will predictably add, which may be an effective way for the Government to convey implicitly messages it may not wish to convey explicitly. Under the headline 'Welfare: the Crackdown', the newspaper report runs as follows:

> Single parents will be forced to take at least a first step towards finding work as Tony Blair cracks down on the benefit culture. A tough new welfare regime, to be unveiled by the Premier today, will make all claimants turn up for job-seeking interviews. People who refuse to help them-selves could have their benefits stopped. The move is the biggest blow so far attempted against the 'something for nothing' mentality that has inflated the cost of the welfare state to £8 billion a year.

The newspaper might reasonably claim that there is nothing here which is not in Blair's article. In terms of propositional content this is arguably so. But the report effects certain transformations which significantly and (from a press officer's perspective) predictably convey a 'tougher' message than Blair's. For instance, he writes of 'a fundamental break with the past' and 'powerful new signals to all benefit applicants', not of a 'crackdown', a small change in wording which however carries an important change of discourse, introducing a discourse of criminality. Blair writes that 'lone parents will have to come for an interview or risk losing their benefits', not of them being 'forced' or 'made' to come – Blair uses a language of obligation which the newspaper 'translates' into a language of coercion. Blair writes of the 'something for nothing days', not of the 'something for nothing mentality', nor of a 'benefit culture' – this introduces a moral critique of the attitudes and lifestyle of welfare claimants which is absent from (or at least more covert in) Blair's article. Moreover, the heavy focus on single parents (in the lead paragraph, but also through the whole report) is the newspaper's rather than Blair's. Of course, the Government cannot be held responsible for what the newspaper writes, but one must ask whether press officers do not strategically anticipate it, and in that sense use the media to convey implicit messages.

These examples are details from a much bigger picture. The whole process of welfare reform has been carefully managed, and this has included careful calculation and control of language. Language has been used to promote the outcomes that the Government is seeking. The precise management of that process has inevitably had the effect of discouraging dialogue and making it more difficult – it is very difficult to engage in real dialogue with someone whose every word is strategically calculated. Discouraging dialogue means discouraging democracy, shifting the process of welfare reform from politics to management.

Consultation as promotion: the welfare reform Green Paper

The Green Paper on welfare reform, published in March 1998, was one of the focal points of the reform process, and the examples I have been discussing so far can be seen as part of preparing the ground for the Green Paper. A Green Paper in the British system of government is a document in which the Government sets out its plans for public consultation and discussion. I want to suggest however that the Green Paper itself is just as carefully managed as the overall reform process, that its language is promotional, and that it is a document which makes real dialogue difficult rather than encouraging it (as it claims to do).

The Green Paper is simultaneously action and representation, part of the business of governing and part the development of a political discourse. It constitutes the 'world of welfare' in a particular way and tells a particular story about how that world can and should be changed; but at the same time it aims to win conviction and support for that picture of welfare and that plan for change.

The Green Paper consists of a (signed) preface by the Prime Minister Tony Blair, followed by a summary of the whole document, chapter 1 which sets out the case for welfare reform, chapter 2 which identifies four 'ages' of welfare and eight 'key principles' of welfare reform which constitute the topics of chapters 3–10. Chapter 11 is about the longer-term future of welfare, and there is an appendix on the evolution of social security. I shall focus on one chapter of the Green Paper (chapter 3: 'The importance of work').

Each of the central chapters (3–10) is structured as follows: a chapter title ('The importance of work' in the case of chapter 3), below which there is a coloured box containing one of the eight 'principles' of the proposed welfare reform. In this case 'Principle 1': *The new welfare state should help and encourage people of working age to work where they are capable of doing so.* There is then an unheaded introductory section focusing on past and present welfare practices, and the case for reform; a section headed 'Policy Direction', taking up the bulk of the chapter (paragraphs 6–40) and setting out proposed future welfare practices; and under the heading 'Measures for Success' a short list of criteria against which the success of the proposed reforms will be judged (end of paragraph 40). Each of the chapters tells readers what the case is for welfare reform but above all what the Government has done, is doing, and intends or aims to do in the way of welfare reform.

In these accounts welfare reform is constructed as a managerial process of problem solving, finding solutions to obstacles in the way of the objectives formulated in the eight 'principles', with the problem-solver represented as virtually exclusively the Government itself. Specifically in chapter 3 the argument goes as follows: work is the means of averting poverty and welfare dependency, but there are obstacles to people working, so the Government will take certain steps to facilitate work. This argumentative structure is repeated in places within the central 'Policy Direction' part of the chapter, though its focus is heavily on the 'solutions' (the predominant type of clause has an actional process with the Government as agent – what the Government has done, is doing, or will do). Representing welfare reform as managerial problem solving and structuring these central chapters of the document in terms of problem solving is part of what makes the genre promotional: the Government's policies are sold as merely technical solutions to what is assumed to be an agreed problem.

Let me refer to two related details of the language of the Green Paper which are indicative of its promotional character – its grammatical mood and its modality (see the Glossary). Although in the nature of things there are many unanswered questions at this consultative stage in the reform process, no questions are asked in chapter 3, and very few questions are asked in the document as a whole. The grammatical mood is overwhelmingly declarative, i.e. overwhelmingly the document (or rather its authors) is telling readers rather than asking them. There is nothing inherent in official documents that requires this – for instance another Green Paper, produced by the Department of Education and Employment (1998), of 'the learning age' asks questions of readers throughout. The potential for questions is indicated too in this Green Paper by their presence at the end of the summary chapter, where the reform process is constructed as debate (I referred to part of this briefly above):

> it is also vital that reform is informed by full debate on the proposed framework. We are consulting widely on the content of this Green Paper and we want your views. For instance, how can we best deliver on our guiding principles? Are there ways in which the policy direction can be improved? Are our tracking measurements for success right?

But there are virtually no further questions in the body of the document. Why not?

Moreover, the many declarative statements are overwhelmingly categorical assertions. Again, although in the nature of things there are uncertainties about what has happened or what is the case and hesitations about what should be done, there are no 'maybes' here. The authors of the document (and by implication the Government) are constructed in the Green Papers as fully knowledgeable, authoritative, and in control. Given the nature of things, it is a simulation of certainty and control, part of the representation of welfare reform as problem solving, and part of the promotional rhetoric of the document.

Taking the two points together, an opportunity for dialogue has been missed. Consider for instance the opening paragraph of chapter 3:

> The Government's aim is to rebuild the welfare state around work. The skills and energies of the workforce are the UK's biggest economic asset. And for both individuals and fami-

lies, paid work is the most secure means of averting poverty and dependence except, of course, for those who are retired or so sick or disabled or so heavily engaged in caring activities, that they cannot realistically support themselves.

There is an implicit argument here – the Government aims to rebuild the welfare state around work first because the UK economy needs those who can work to do so, second because paid work is the best way of averting poverty and dependence. The authors might have presented the Government's argument as one contribution (if an influential one) to a dialogue, perhaps as follows:

> The Government's aim is to rebuild the welfare state around work. We have adopted this policy because we believe the UK economy needs the skills and energies of all those who can work (these are the UK's biggest economic asset), and because we believe that for both individuals and families paid work is the more secure means of averting poverty and dependence. Do you agree?

This differs from the original in making the argument explicit but also in mood (including a question) and modality (including a marker of 'subjective modality', 'we believe', which acknowledges that this is one view amongst others).

It strikes me that there is a constant slippage in the Green Paper between the process of consultation over proposed welfare reform, and a sort of anticipation of the implementation of the policy once it has been agreed. It is partly a consultation document, but also partly the sort of document that is used in planning how to actually do things once they are agreed. Welfare reform is not simply represented as problem solving in the document, it actually enacts problem solving. This is evident in the use of 'boxes' (eight in all) in chapter 3 and throughout the document. These are parts of the text that are in a different colour from the rest and which are made up of 'bullet points' (or sometimes numbered points), often with headings. Such boxes are widely used in planning documents. The clearest example of this sort of use is at the end of the chapter, the 'Success Measures':

Success Measures

1   A reduction in the proportion of working age people living in workless households.

2 A reduction in the proportion of working age people out of work for more than two years.

3 An increase in the number of working age people in work.

4 An increase in the proportion of lone parents, people with a long-term illness and disabled people of working age in touch with the labour market.

This is all there is on 'success measures' in the chapter – there is no discussion of what the 'success measures' should be, and not even a statement of the form: 'The measures of our success in achieving our objectives should be as follows ...' All we have is this list, as if this were an internal government document informating civil servants how the new system will work. The Green Paper is jumping ahead of the consultation process, which hardly encourages dialogue.

These boxes figure as a structuring device for the document. For instance, the box in paragraph 5 of chapter 3 (which I briefly commented on in the Introduction) lists in their sequential order the main sections of the 'Policy Direction' part of the chapter, which takes up 35 of its 40 paragraphs.

5 The Government aims to promote work by:

– helping people move from welfare to work through the New Deals and Employment Zones;

– developing flexible personalised services to help people into work;

– lowering the barriers to work for those who can and want to work;

– making work pay, by reforming the tax and benefit system, including a Working Families Tax Credit, reforming National Insurance and income tax, and introducing the national minimum wage; and

– ensuring that responsibilities and rights are fairly matched.

Such boxes are part of the strong unilateral control of the text and attempted control of the reader exercised by the authors. One might say that they are 'reader-friendly', helping the reader with the reading process by setting out the main points and, in this case, the basic structure of the chapter in a clear, digestible way. That may be so, but the downside of being 'reader-friendly' is being 'reader-directive', guiding and controlling the way the reader sees the issues, and, in this case, sees the document. 'Reader-friendly' texts tend to narrow the reader's options – of course it remains possible to resist direction, but it takes an effort to do so. The boxes are in a sense pedagogical – they construct the author (and by implication the Government) as the knowledgeable teacher and the reader as the learner (such boxes are widely used in educational texts). They are also promotional. Their helpful clarity is persuasive – such boxes are also widely used in advertising. What may appear to be an apparently innocent, purely technical, presentational device carries a social and ideological ballast. I believe that it does not encourage dialogue.

Throughout the document, there is an 'oscillation', a to-ing-and-fro-ing, between informing and persuading, or as one might put it between 'telling' and 'selling'. Correspondingly there is an oscillation between the social relations of telling (the one who knows and the one who doesn't, the teacher and the learner) and the social relations of 'selling' (the one who sells and the one who potentially buys). We can take paragraph 5 (see above) and the two immediately following paragraphs as an example:

6   The Government's biggest investment since taking office has been in a large-scale welfare to work programme. Our ambition is nothing less than a change of culture among benefit claimants, employers and public servants – with rights and responsibilities on all sides. Those making the shift from welfare to work will be provided with positive assistance, not just a benefit payment.

7   Our comprehensive welfare to work programme aims to break the mould of the old, passive benefit system. It is centred on the five aspects of the New Deal ...

One aspect of the oscillation is the shift between third person ('the Government', paragraph 5, the first and third sentences of paragraph 6, the second sentence of paragraph 7) and first person ('we', the second sentence of paragraph 6, the first sentence of paragraph 7). This oscillation between 'the Government' and 'we' occurs throughout the document in the 'solutions' part of the problem-solution structure. Notice that 'we' is open to an ambivalence which is an aspect of the promotional character of the genre – for instance, is the 'we' of 'our ambition' in paragraph 6 the Government, or the Labour Party? And, more generally, is the Green Paper government report, or party 'propaganda'? Another aspect of the oscillation between informing and persuading is the shift in explicitness of evaluation. The two sentences with first person are also the two most explicitly evaluative – the first including the noun 'ambition', which has a marked positive evaluation in contrast with 'aim' (which occurs here twice as a verb), and 'nothing less than'; the second including several words/expressions which are positively evaluative ('comprehensive', 'break the mould') or negatively evaluative ('old', 'passive') in this context.

How does the Green Paper represent the 'world of welfare' – the activities and processes which constitute the welfare system, including the process of welfare reform itself? I want to argue that its representation is univocal, that it includes only one perspective, one voice – that of the Government itself. This univocality is textually evident in the rarity of reported speech in the document. There are many positions and perspectives within the world of welfare, and correspondingly various views on the process of welfare reform, but the representation of the world of welfare reduces its population to virtually two major participants: the Government and the claimants. Welfare staff feature very little, claimants' organisations and campaign groups hardly at all, and welfare professionals and experts never. One might say that an obvious opportunity for dialogue, which would seem to accord with the declared objectives of this consultation document, has been foregone – the opportunity to give voice to a range of perspectives on welfare and welfare reform. The document could have 'given voice' to a whole range of perspectives and positions within the world of welfare by quoting what people have said about welfare reform. But that would hardly fit in with its apparent primary concern to promote the Government's proposals.

It is instructive, however, to look at some of those rare points in the document where reported speech and thought do occur. The following is a paragraph from the third chapter:

> Lone parent organisations, employers and lone parents themselves have all welcomed this New Deal, and the staff responsible for delivering the service have been particularly enthusiastic. The staff have welcomed the opportunity to become involved in providing practical help and advice. The first phase of this New Deal has aroused considerable interest: lone parents in other parts of the country are asking if they can join in.

There is also a scatter of other examples of reported thought elsewhere in the chapter, where claimants are subjects of mental process verbs (e.g. 'the vast majority of single parents want to work', 'some people feel forced to give up their job'). Sometimes when we have reported speech the context and social practice within which it occurred is explicitly identified. Here it is not. But it seems that this reported speech comes from market research (opinion polls, surveys, perhaps focus groups). In fact, it seems that the only practice, which is reported in the document in terms of what claimants (and staff) say or think, is market research. Notice in particular the way in which thought is reported. For example, in 'the vast majority of single parents want to work' not only is the practice where these 'wants' were expressed unspecified, so also is who expressed them. (A possible alternative might be: 'in a poll of single parent opinion, the vast majority of those asked said they wanted to work'.) The Government takes it upon itself to speak for these people. One might say that this form of governance includes market research as a technology for legitimising the Government speaking for the public. Apart from these examples, the voices of others (including relevant others such as welfare professionals and claimant groups) are not reported.

The Government's welfare reform policy is summed up as 'welfare to work', getting people off welfare and into work, so the practice of work is constantly referred to but in highly selective ways. Here again the document goes for promotion rather than dialogue. It could have made itself more dialogical by including many diverse representations of work, many different discourses of work, but instead it monologically privileges one discourse of work. A key issue is what is seen as included within the practice of work – what 'work' is. Work is overwhelmingly constructed in the document as 'jobs' in the traditional sense – relatively stable and regular work providing enough to live on. The fact that an increasing proportion of work is casual, part-time, and poorly paid is not focused on in the document. Nor is the question of whether, for example, women's work in households counts as 'work'. Recent debate over what should count as 'work' does not figure – whether, for example, governments should deliberately stimulate the 'third' (e.g. voluntary) sector and legitimise it as 'work'.[23] Although other discourses of work are not explicitly included, they do have an implicit presence. (Recall the description in chapter 2 of the word 'work' in the New Labour corpus.)

For the most part, the word 'work' is used without modification to mean 'jobs' in the sense above. However, there is a shift to the expression 'paid work' twice in the document, once in paragraph 1 of chapter 3 (see above, pp. 134–5). Why this shift? It is significant that it occurs at the beginning of the chapter dealing centrally with work.

The shift is informationally backgrounded – 'paid work' in sentence 3 is constructed as simply a repetition of 'work' in sentence 1. There is no explicit contrast between paid and other sorts of work. Nevertheless, the shift does implicitly signal a contrast – the specification of 'work' as 'paid work' is an implicit acknowledgement that there are other understandings (and discourses) of work. There is also a trace of an alternative discourse of 'work' later in the chapter in paragraph 9, which is the only such case in the document. A list of 'opportunities' for young unemployed people includes: 'work with an employer who will receive a job subsidy', 'work with a voluntary sector organisation', and 'work on the Environmental Taskforce'. Only the first is a 'job' in the usual sense. On the other hand, when the document refers to what parents do in caring for children, it does not refer to that activity as 'work'. As with reported speech so with discourses, an important variable is whether they are attributed (to voices) and located (in practices). What we have here is a covert recontextualisation of what people say about work in other practices (not of specific things they say – not reported speech as above – but more abstractly of their discourse), which neither attributes nor locates this discourse.

The Green Paper is cut off from debates over the nature and future of work through the exclusion of relevant other voices, and in the dominance of one discourse of work over an alternative that is only covert, and other alternatives that are totally absent. Yet one might think that these debates are crucial for a policy which depends entirely on moving people from welfare into work, given that the number of 'jobs' in the traditional sense is shrinking. Without some fundamental rethinking of the nature of work, the policy looks at best incoherent, at worst dishonest.

By contrast with the representation of work, there is a diversity of discourses in the representation of the social relations of welfare within the document. That diversity is evident to a degree in the introductory section of this chapter, specifically in paragraph 5, which includes the following representations of the practices of the new world of welfare: 'promote work', 'help people move from welfare to work' (and, in Principle 1, 'help and encourage people to work'), 'develop flexible … services', 'responsibilities and rights are fairly matched'. The construction of the social relations of welfare as 'helping' relations has been central to the British welfare state, but 'helping' is mainly focused in this document on getting people off welfare and into work. 'Promoting' and 'developing flexible … services' by contrast belong to a managerial discourse, and the former connotes cultural intervention. There is also legal/contractual discourse in 'responsibilities and rights'.

But the main feature of the construction of the social relations of welfare is the mixture of bureaucratic/professional welfare discourse ('helping' etc.) and managerial/cultural ('promoting' etc.), with the latter predominant. An example of the latter is in paragraph 21 of chapter 3: 'personalised', 'flexible' services are 'delivered' through a single 'gateway' for 'customers' by 'personal advisers' who develop 'tailor-made action plans' for individuals. There is a new discourse here which 'relexicalises'[24] welfare services, gives them a new vocabulary. Cultural effects can be achieved in so far as the Government can win acceptance for such shifts in discourse and the new identities and values they entail. The diversity of discourses here in contrast with the representation of work is probably due to the fact the Government is trying to shift from one construction of the social relations of welfare to another.

Summing up, I have suggested that the Green Paper is itself just as promotional as the overall welfare reform process of which it is a part, and that in a variety of ways it avoids dialogue and makes dialogue difficult.

6

RHETORIC AND REALITY

Kosovo

Matthew Taylor, head of the pro-Labour think-tank, the Institute for Public Policy Research, calling for 'more constructive but critical engagement' by the left with the New Labour Government, has claimed that:[1]

> You can't understand New Labour unless you get to grips with the reality–rhetoric dichotomy. This is the left's big opportunity? Where the rhetoric is conservative but the reality radical fiscal redistribution, the left should sing the government's praises, celebrating the pursuit of social justice. When the rhetoric is ambitious but the reality less convincing (ending poverty, making work family-friendly) the left should show how the vision can be matched by action without committing political suicide.

Taylor points to gaps between rhetoric and reality in two directions. On the one hand, there is the familiar case (which I discussed in the Introduction) of 'rhetoric' in the sense of empty words, 'mere words', where what the Government does fails to match up to what it says (though Taylor puts a rather benign construction on this, as if rhetoric in this sense were only failing to achieve a laudable ambition – see below). On the other hand, there is the rather less obvious case of the Government's actions going further than its words. What Taylor is alluding to here is a widespread (though contentious) interpretation of the economic policies of the Chancellor of the Exchequer, Gordon Brown. Brown has introduced several measures, which are widely seen as having the effect of redistributing wealth in favour of the poor, although the political discourse of New Labour excludes such a redistributionist strategy. Examples are the increase in child benefit, the Working Family Tax Credit, and the Child Care Tax Credit. A common explanation for this gap between rhetoric and reality is that it is designed to keep middle-class support – that New Labour is pursuing, to a degree at least, traditional Labour policies that benefit the working class, but disguising what it is doing so as not to upset the middle class.

Whether or not this interpretation of what Brown is doing and of his motivation for doing it covertly is plausible, it does point to the importance of asking how the rhetoric compares to the reality – a question which has come up at various points in the book. But we can only do so if we have a framework of analysis that provides a coherent way of (a) distinguishing the rhetoric from the reality, as well as (b) showing the relationship between the rhetoric and the reality. The point is simple: if we can't distinguish rhetoric from reality, there's no way of comparing them, asking if there are gaps between them of the sort discussed above.

Since the point is rather obvious, why is it an issue? In the Introduction I put forward an argument for a book about the politics of New Labour that focuses on language. The argument was that not only is language inherently important in politics and government, but changes in politics and government associated with New Labour are making it more important. So, politics and government as discourse? Such a perspective fits in with the 'turn to discourse' in recent social analysis, which has meant that many aspects of social life come to be analysed as discourse in many disciplines – for instance sociology and psychology as well as politics.[2] While I welcome this widespread recognition of the importance of discourse in social life, it carries a risk: taking the argument too far so that social life comes to be seen as nothing but discourse.[3]

Discourse and social practices

The aim of this book is not theoretical – it is not to discuss theories of discourse, or methods analysing discourse. Nevertheless, I do need to explain how I see discourse analysis in order to take a coherent position on the important question of rhetoric and reality in New Labour. I shall briefly discuss this with reference to government as a 'social practice'.

I see government as a social practice, meaning a particular area of social life which is structured in a distinctive way involving particular groups of people (politicians, public employees, welfare claimants, the general public, and so on) in particular relations with each other. Of course, the social practice of government changes – I have been emphasising the changes that are associated with New Labour in this book – and its relationship to other social practices (e.g. the mass media or voluntary work) changes. Nevertheless, it roughly sustains over long periods of time its identity as one area of social life in contrast with others.

Every social practice holds diverse elements of social life together within a sort of network. These elements include physical elements (e.g. the bodily actions of people and the physical environments within which they take place), broadly sociological elements (institutional and organisational structures, procedures, rituals, and so forth – such as institutional aspects of the political system), broadly psychological elements (bodies of knowledge, beliefs, attitudes, feelings, etc.) – and language (in a broad sense, including the semiotics of, for instance, bodily movement and gesture and of visual images, as well as language). Summing this up as a diagram:

Elements of a social practice

physical
sociological
psychological
language

Clearly one could argue about how to categorise the various elements of practices, but that is not a central issue here. The main point is that language is just one element of any practice, including the practice of government. Government includes physical elements (including, for instance, physical force which the police or armed forces use), sociological elements in a broad sense (e.g. the political system), psychological elements (knowledge, beliefs, attitudes, etc.) – and language.

These elements are different from each other, but they are not discrete – what I mean by that is that they affect each other and inflect each other. Even the physical force enacted by an army does not exclude language: armies apply force according to military doctrines, strategies, and tactics, which are constituted in language. In a reasonable sense we can say that actions on the battlefield have particular discourses 'internalised' within them.[4] Or, to take an example closer to the concerns of this book, the behaviour of public employees in welfare departments in their contacts with claimants has particular discourses 'internalised' within it. New Labour shows some awareness of this – it sets out to change their behaviours by changing the language (e.g. constructing claimants as 'customers'). But if these elements are not discrete, they are still different. The fact that the physical force applied by an army internalises particular discourses does *not* of course mean that it is just discourse. So the idea of 'internalisation' is a way of recognising the pervasive effects of language in shaping social life, without falling into the trap I referred to above of saying that social life is nothing but discourse.[5]

How does the distinction between 'rhetoric' and 'reality' fit in to this? Recall the distinction I made in the Introduction between three aspects of the language of New Labour (and in fact of language in any social practice): genres, discourses, and styles. Language figures in broadly three ways in social life. First, language is part of the action, so to speak – part of the activity that goes on in the social practice (part of the process of governing in this case). A particular way of governing involves particular ways of using language – *genres*. Second, language represents the action – in this case, the political *discourse* of New Labour represents social life generally and governing in particular in specific ways. Third, language is part of the performance, part of the way in which particular people perform in particular positions in the practice. A particular way of performing (e.g. Tony Blair's way of being Prime Minister) goes with a particular *style*.[6]

When Taylor wrote about the 'reality–rhetoric dichotomy' he was referring to the relationship between the action and the political discourse of New Labour – between what New Labour does, and what it says it does. But there are also two other ways of understanding the 'reality–rhetoric dichotomy' in terms of the framework above. First, as the dichotomy between language as part of the action and other parts of the action. For instance, what the Government did when it increased child benefit included Gordon Brown making an announcement in Parliament, and the production of official documents specifying the new regulations. Yet there might be a gap between these linguistic parts of the action and others if, for instance, the Government failed to ensure increased child benefits were actually delivered to those who qualified for them. Second, as the dichotomy between style and substance, perhaps between how a politician performs publicly and what s/he does behind the scenes, between constructed and real (less savoury) identity. I shall continue referring to the 'reality–rhetoric dichotomy' because it is such a convenient shorthand, but I am also suggesting some rather complex relationships between elements and aspects of a social practice.

Political discourse and political pragmatism: freedom of information

I said above that Taylor puts a rather benign construction on cases where Government action fails to match up with Government discourse. It's not always a matter of laudable ambition that could not be fulfilled, it's sometimes a matter of less creditable backtracking to protect vested interests. A case in point is the Government's Freedom of Information Bill. Before becoming Prime Minister, Tony Blair spoke about freedom of information as follows:

> Our commitment to a freedom of information act is clear, and I reaffirm it here tonight. We want to end the obsessive and unnecessary secrecy which surrounds government activity and make government information available to the public unless there are good reasons not to do so. So the presumption is that information should be, rather than should not be, released ...
>
> Information relating to national security, to law enforcement, to commercial confidentiality, to personal privacy, should of course be subject to exemption, as should the policy advice given by civil servants to ministers ...
>
> A freedom of information act would signal a cultural change that would make a dramatic difference to the way that Britain is governed. The very fact of its introduction would signal a new relationship between government and people: a relationship which sees the public as legitimate stakeholders in the running of the country and sees election to serve the public as being given on trust.
>
> I believe in the programme of constitutional change that the Labour party has outlined. I think that a freedom of information act is an important and essential part of that ... It is genuinely about changing the relationship in politics today.
>
> There is so much disaffection from politics, so much disillusion with it, and one of the very simple reasons is that we live in a modern and far better educated and far more open and far more assertive democracy and country – and it is good that people feel that way.
>
> The irony is that the system of government is about 50, 60, 70 years behind the actual feelings and sentiments of the broad majority of people. A freedom of information act is

not just important itself. It is part of bringing our politics up to date.[7]

Blair works the Freedom of Information Bill into the political discourse of the 'Third Way' at a stage where 'stakeholding' was a key element of that discourse ('the public as legitimate stakeholders in the running of the country', see chapter 3). This passage evokes the 'Third Way' themes of a 'new politics' ('changing the relationship in politics today') and the 'modernisation' of Britain ('bringing our politics up to date'). Yet when the draft Bill was published in May 1999 it provoked a storm of protest because it was seen as a betrayal by a government eager to preserve in office the 'obsessive secrecy' it had denounced in opposition. A White Paper published in 1997 had incorporated New Labour's earlier radical position. Attention therefore focused on the changes that had been made between the White Paper and the Bill, in particular, the dropping of the requirement that authorities wanting to withhold information must demonstrate that release would cause 'substantial harm'. Instead, they would only have to show that disclosure would 'prejudice' the workings of government. There are also more exemptions than in the White Paper, more cases where there is no requirement at all to show 'prejudice', including information obtained by safety agencies investigating accidents, and information which 'relates to the formulation or development of government policy' – not only sensitive policy advice, but also factual information (such as scientific advice on genetically modified food).

The gap between rhetoric and reality in this case is the gap between the language of the Bill and the language of New Labour's political discourse about the Bill – being able to withhold information on the grounds that it would 'prejudice' the workings of government is not consistent with, in Blair's terms, 'the presumption that information should be released'. So the gap between rhetoric and reality in this case is not between language and something else – it is between language used in one place and language used in another: language used in political discourse and language used in government action.

Rhetoric and truth: Kosovo

The example above belongs to a significant category of gaps between rhetoric and reality (or discourse and action) in government: unkept promises. My second example is rather more akin to the claim discussed above that Gordon Brown's actions have redistributed wealth in a way that is at odds with the political discourse of New Labour – it appears to involve a rhetoric which disguises reality. It is a rather less favourable example.

Tony Blair represented the NATO bombing of the Yugoslav Republic in the spring and early summer of 1999 as 'a just and moral cause' (the *Sun*, 4 June 1999), 'a just war, based not on any territorial ambitions but on values':

> We cannot let the evil of ethnic cleansing stand. We must not rest until it is reversed. We have learned twice before in this century that appeasement does not work. If we let an evil dictator range unchallenged, we will have to spill infinitely more blood and treasure to stop him later.[8]

I discussed this extract in chapter 4 as an example of 'Blair the wartime leader', analysing it as a combination of moral righteousness and toughness. The extract comes from an important speech on the 'doctrine of the international community' which Blair gave in Chicago on the eve of the NATO 50th anniversary meeting in Washington, during the middle of the bombing campaign. It was Blair's righteousness and toughness that received most attention in media reports. Indeed, throughout the bombing Blair was prominently presented not only in the British media but also in North America and other parts of Europe as the toughest advocate amongst NATO leaders of pursuing what he consistently portrayed as a war for humanitarian motives by whatever means were necessary.

Yet the speech contains other elements which begin to provide, so to speak, 'internal evidence' of a gap between rhetoric and reality – raising the question of whether the war was about more than humanitarian relief. Blair summed up the concerns of the speech as follows: 'I want to speak to you this evening about events in Kosovo. But I want to put these events in a wider context – economic, political, security – because I do not believe Kosovo can be seen in isolation.' The wider context for Kosovo was according to Blair 'globalisation', which imposes 'global interdependence' in the economic, political, and security domains, and requires 'us' to focus 'on the principles of the doctrine of international community and on the institutions that deliver them'. (Blair proposes a number of issues that 'we' should address, but the nature of these 'principles' is left vague.) The speech is 'dedicated to the cause of internationalism and against isolationism'. The 'internationalism' Blair is advocating (giving that word a very different sense to that of workers' solidarity, which it has traditionally had in the Labour movement) includes the three domains of 'global interdependence', and the main sections of the speech deal with them in turn: economic, security, and political interdependence.

With respect to economic globalisation, Blair calls for 'a thorough, far-reaching overhaul and reform of the system of international financial regulation', and 'a new push on free trade in the WTO' (the World Trade Organisation). International community means 'accepting the judgements of international organisations even when you do not like them'.

The section on 'security' begins: 'The principles of international community apply also to international security.' Blair then says of the decade since the end of the Cold War, 'our armed forces have been busier than ever' and that 'many of our problems have been caused by two dangerous and ruthless men – Saddam Hussein and Slobodan Milosevic'. Who 'we' are is not specified. The speech continues:

> One of the reasons why it is now so important to win the conflict is to ensure that others do not make the same mistake in the future. That in itself will be a major step to ensuring that the next decade and the next century will not be as difficult as the past. If NATO fails in Kosovo, the next dictator to be threatened with military force may well not believe our resolve to carry the threat through.
>
> At the end of this century the US has emerged as by far the strongest state. It has no dreams of world conquest and is not seeking colonies. If anything Americans are too ready to see no need to get involved in affairs of the rest of the world. America's allies are always both relieved and gratified by its continuing readiness to shoulder burdens and responsibilities which come with its sole superpower status. We understand that this is something that we have no right to take for granted, and must match with our own efforts. This is the basis for the recent initiative I took with President Chirac of France to improve Europe's own defence capabilities.
>
> As we address these problems at this weekend's NATO Summit we may be tempted to think back to the clarity and simplicity of the Cold War. But now we have to establish a new framework. No longer is our existence as states under threat. Now our actions are guided by a more subtle blend

of mutual self-interest and moral purpose in defending the values we cherish. In the end values and interests merge. If we can establish and spread the values of liberty, the rule of law, human rights and an open society then that is in our national interests too. The spread of our values makes us safer. As John Kennedy put it 'Freedom is indivisible and when one man is enslaved who is free?'

The most pressing foreign policy problem we face is to identify the circumstances in which we should get actively involved in other people's conflicts.

Blair then goes on to propose 'five major considerations' in deciding 'when and whether we will intervene'.

The third section is politics. The 'Third Way' is defined now in international terms as 'an attempt by centre and centre-left Governments to re-define a political programme that is neither old left nor 1980s right'. The 'new political agenda we stand for' is summarised as: (1) 'financial prudence as the foundation of economic success', (2) a new economic role for Government … not picking winners, heavy handed intervention, old-style corporatism, but: education, skills, technology, small business entrepreneurship', (3) 'reforming welfare systems and public services', (4) 'tough on crime, tough on the causes of crime', (5) 'reinventing or reforming Government itself'.

And 'the final thing we all have in common, the new centre, centre-left Governments, is we are internationalists'. Blair goes on to set out a British position which is 'both pro-Europe and pro-America', rejecting 'the false proposition that we must choose', and which involves 'the battle for economic reform in Europe' ('to ensure flexible labour markets, to remove the regulatory burdens, and to untie the hands of business') – the 'Third Way in Europe', preventing 'the European Union becoming a closed fortress'.

I have gone into some detail about the content and organisation of the speech because I think what is significant about it is the way it weaves different domains of government (and different discourses) together, and the way it does so only becomes clear when we look at the speech as a whole. It does so through a particular construction of 'globalisation' as comprising three domains: economy, security, and politics. It uses 'globalisation' as a frame within which to connect these three domains, and it invites us to see Kosovo in terms of their connection – 'I want to speak to you this evening about events in Kosovo. But I want to put these events in a wider context –

economic, political, security – because I do not believe Kosovo can be seen in isolation'. Indeed, 'twenty years ago we would not have been fighting in Kosovo. We would have turned our backs on it. The fact that we are engaged is the result of ... globalisation.' So it is clear from Blair's speech: the NATO intervention in Yugoslavia has to be seen as part of a new reality, which connects the global economy, international security, and international politics.

I began this section by saying that the speech appears to involve a rhetoric which disguises reality. Yet on one level the speech points to a reality which was largely missing from the rhetoric of the media coverage of the Yugoslav war. For instance, reports of this speech in the American media focused mainly on Blair's tough moral stance, picking up soundbites such as 'this is a just war', as well as Blair's list of 'considerations' for deciding when NATO should intervene. They did not take up interconnections between economy, security, and politics in a globalised world. But on another level the speech itself leaves a gap between rhetoric and reality. It may 'point to' a reality which was largely missing from media coverage, but it 'points to' it without being explicit about it, without really explaining what it is. We might say that it raises more questions than it answers. When it comes to the nature of the connections between economy, security, and politics, it is just vague.

Let me show this in terms of discourses. Corresponding to its construction of globalisation as having three areas, the speech weaves together three different discourses: a discourse of 'international security', a discourse of economic globalisation, and the political discourse of the 'Third Way' (which in the process is projected as an international discourse). One particular and crucial vagueness which arises in the articulation of these three discourses is the identity of the 'we': Who is Blair talking about when he says 'we have to co-operate with each other across nations'? (Recall the discussion of 'we' in chapter 1.) 'We' means different things in the three different discourses, and the speech says nothing about how these differences can be reconciled. In the discourse of 'international security', 'we' seems to be NATO: 'If NATO fails in Kosovo, the next dictator to be threatened with military force may well not believe our resolve to carry the threat through.' In the discourse of economic globalisation, 'we' seems to be sometimes the G7 countries ('I hope the Summit [of G7 Finance Ministers] will go further too in the case of Russia. We simply cannot stand back and watch that great nation teeter on the brink of ruin.'), and sometimes a vaguely inclusive but undefined grouping of nations ('we need to modernise the international financial architecture'). 'We' also sometimes refers to Britain in particular. In the political discourse of the 'Third Way', 'we' is governments of the centre, centre-left – it is explicitly glossed as such: 'the final thing we have in common, the new centre, centre-left Governments, is we are internationalists'. So 'we' (apart from when the reference is specifically to Britain) slides between NATO, G7, the 'new centre, centre-left Governments' who are oriented to the notion of the 'Third Way', as well as a more inclusive but undefined grouping of nations. The title of the speech ('Doctrine of the international community') refers to 'the international community' as if it were something well-defined (it presupposes that there is an international community), yet what we get in the speech is a series of disjunctions between different 'communities' referred to as 'we'.

Yet it seems that, despite the disjunctions, most people were able to interpret what Blair was saying as coherent – reports and commentaries on the speech did not ask: 'What on earth does Blair mean?' It seems that people could see what he was getting at, and see what he meant by 'the international community', by 'we'. How is that possible given the disjunctions in the meaning of 'we'? Because people can imply more than they actually say – and in this case many people hearing or reading the speech could see Blair as implying more than he actually said about who the 'we' is. Roughly speaking, he seems to be implying that the small group of states defined by the intersection of the three discourses, the states which are members of NATO and of G7 and have 'centre, centre-left Governments' (USA, Britain, Germany, France, and so forth) can be seen as standing for 'the international community' in the sense of the community of all nation-states. This is taken for granted as a sort of common sense, a sort of unspoken hierarchy which we all understand: a small number of the richest and most powerful countries stand for, represent, act on behalf of, etc., the rest. What I am suggesting is that in order to make sense of the concept of 'the international community', which is the focus of Blair's speech, in order to arrive at a coherent interpretation which irons out the disjunctions in the meaning of 'we', we have to assume something along these lines.

As a common-sense assumption this is usually unproblematic and goes unquestioned – it can be taken for granted as 'the way of the world'. But imagine what would happen if Blair were to explicitly propose such an elitist understanding of 'the international community' as part of his doctrine. It would probably cause uproar because it would make explicit an aspect of 'the way of the world' which depends upon being kept implicit, at least in the language of politicians like Blair. It's not that we don't know such things – many of us will have watched some TV programme or read some newspaper article about iniquitous inequalities between states. It is rather that such knowledge is compartmentalised; it is retained in one corner of people's heads and repressed most of the time.[9] But as soon as we see this as the 'unsaid' in Blair's speech, as soon as we formulate it explicitly as I have done above, it opens up the gap I referred to earlier between the rhetoric of the speech and the reality of the NATO intervention. It 'points to' the reality in a way which highlights the vagueness of what Blair is saying, the questions he leaves unanswered. What after all is the link between the economic power, the military might, and the political agenda of the states which stand for and act for the wider international community? Were there not for instance undeclared economic or strategic interests underlying the NATO intervention? Blair does not even suggest that this is a question to be asked, yet the way he superimposes the three communities of the G7 states, NATO, and the 'centre, centre-left Governments' to constitute the elite of 'the international community' nevertheless points us to that question.

The suspicious question I have just asked is alluded to in the extract I gave above from the section on 'security', only to be dismissed: '[the US] has no dreams of world conquest and is not seeking colonies'. Yet this evades the question of the covert self-interest of the USA by casting it in archaic terms: relationships of dependency and subordination may have been achieved through conquest and colonisation in the nineteenth century, but at the turn of the twenty-first century they are achieved more through the operations of the World Bank and the IMF. This paragraph is built around a personification of relationships between states as relationships between friends, and the dubious assumption that states within international relations act like friends who are prepared to 'shoulder responsibilities' and not 'take for granted' what others do for them. This is a very common metaphor, but a deeply misleading one. In this case it is a vehicle for constructing the USA as benign in its international relations, a way of deflecting the sort of suspicious question I asked above.

The next paragraph actually acknowledges 'self-interest', but in a classically New Labour 'not only but also' formulation – self-interest can be reconciled with moral values: 'Now our actions are guided by a subtle blend of mutual self-interest and moral purpose in defending the values we cherish. In the end, values and interests merge.' Yet a close look at the series of the verbs which take 'values' as their object itself suggests we should be suspicious about the optimistic rhetoric of the 'Third Way'. Whereas 'defending' values may seem a fine and moral thing to do, 'spreading' values smacks of the nineteenth century empires alluded to earlier: achieving economic and political control in the name of bringing enlightenment. Whether 'the spread of our values makes us safer' rather depends on whether one's state is positioned inside or outside the elusive 'us'.

The first paragraph of the extract sets 'us' against 'the other': it sets up a division between 'us' ('NATO') and 'the next dictator to be threatened with military force'. The world is simplistically divided in Blair's speech into 'us' and 'the dictators', 'goodies' and 'baddies'. (Milosevic is in fact an elected leader, even if an unsavoury one, who still depends upon parliamentary support.) Moreover, it is implied that 'we' shall continue to pose military threats to 'dictators'. Given the vagueness about who 'we' are, the constitution of 'us' around an elite core, and the fact that a significant part of the world (notably China) firmly dissociated itself from the NATO action, the division of the world into 'us' and the rest and the demonisation of the latter as 'dictators' is a potentially dangerous rhetorical distortion of reality.

I have been suggesting that the rhetoric of Blair's speech at once points to a reality framing the NATO intervention, which is more complex than the media coverage suggested, and obfuscates that reality – constructs it in misleading ways, or leaves it extremely vague. But if that reality is potentially as explosive as I have suggested, why did Blair's speech even hint at it at all? Because the speech was a move towards constituting a new reality, a new doctrine of the international community, which as he points out would also entail 'reformed international institutions'. This process of change in doctrines, rules, and institutions begins in language: it begins with the constitution of a new discourse, a new mix of economic, security, and political discourses, which can construct this wider change in doctrines and institutions, give it a linguistic shape which people can be asked to support. To do this, the language has to show aspects of the reality of the Yugoslav intervention which were not shown in the media coverage of it. But at the same time it cannot show them too clearly because that would be dangerous, that could undermine NATO's public construction of the war – it has to resort to vagueness and implicitness. So what I am suggesting is that Blair's speech is positioned in a contradictory way which sets up a tension in the relationship between language and reality. Language is simultaneously revealing and disguising reality.

When I say language is disguising reality, I am not suggesting that there is a reality 'out there' which we can all see if we simply look in the right way. All we have are different representations of reality, drawing on different discourses. But that does not mean that all representations and discourses are equally good. They are still representations *of* something, and while no one can get at the 'something' except through representations of it, the 'something' nevertheless still exists separately from the representations. People are constantly evaluating different representations, and looking for better ones. We don't usually do this abstractly, merely as a matter of speculation, we usually do it practically, in the course of trying to get something done, which entails working on (often trying to change) the 'something'. That applies also to politics. People are working and competing to change particular things as they are in particular directions, and the question of which representations best fit reality mostly arises in such practical contexts. So talking about a gap between rhetoric and reality is a shorthand way of questioning particular representations of reality – suggesting in this case that Blair's representation of reality is not as good as others (perhaps, for instance, those in a special issue of *New Left Review* devoted to the war).[10]

Rhetoric, reality, and resistance

The Taylor quotation with which I started this chapter linked the 'reality–rhetoric dichotomy' with the left becoming a more effective opposition to New Labour. The political intervention of the left is seen as responses to different types of gaps between rhetoric and reality: 'where the rhetoric is conservative but the reality [of what the Government is doing] radical, the left should sing the government's praises, celebrating the pursuit of social justice. When the rhetoric is ambitious but the reality less convincing … the left should show how the vision can be matched by action without committing political suicide.' This is a matter of doing what I was referring to in the last paragraph – contesting representations of reality, offering and searching for better representations, in the course of practical politics, working and competing to change things in particular directions.

The 'reality–rhetoric dichotomy' provides a basis for political contestation and resistance. Part of what makes politics possible and inevitable is the fact that gaps arise between rhetoric and reality, and become visible to people. The politics of language, the politics of the gaps between reality and rhetoric, is a fundamental part of politics, and it includes the various types of gap I began to distinguish earlier in the chapter – between what people say and what they do, between action which is linguistic and action which takes other forms, between what people implicitly claim they are through their styles of performing and what other evidence suggest they really are. Political opposition to New Labour focuses on all these types of gap – setting, for instance, the discourse of 'partnership' against how New Labour actually governs, new welfare or pensions regulations against the experiences of claimants, or Blair's relaxed and inclusive style against evidence of 'control-freakery'.

Conclusion: How important is language?

How important is language in the analysis of politics and government? According to what I said about social practices at the beginning of chapter 6, language is a part of every social practice. First, there is no social practice whose activity excludes language – language is always part of the action, the question of 'genre' always arises. Why? Because social action is always interaction ('inter-action'), and interaction always involves communication, hence language and other types of semiotic activity. But, second, there is no action without reflection: social action always includes not only representation of the world which constitutes its context and frame, but also reflexive self-representations, representations by the people involved in the action of what they are doing. So, discourses are an inherent part of all social practices. Summing up, social practices always involve language in a combination of action and reflection, genres and discourses. They also involve language in the construction of identities – styles.

So what is special about politics and government? The crucial point is that although language is always an element of a social practice, it can be a more or less important element, a more or less salient part of the practice. Language is a more salient part of certain social practices than of others, and the relative salience of language in a social practice can change. So what I am claiming is (a) that politics and government are social practices in which language is salient – this is a durable feature of these social practices in comparison with others, (b) language is becoming more salient within these practices.

A comparison will help make the point. Language is an element of the social practice of agriculture no less than it is of the social practice of government. But agricultural work – the action of this social practice – is largely physical work. This does not of course mean that it excludes language, because agricultural work is still social, interactive, and therefore communicative – people work together, and their work together is partly language. So we still need to look at the genres of agriculture, even if language is a relatively small part of the action – language has more of a supportive or enabling role than it does in government, where much of the action *is* language. On the other hand, agricultural work, like any work, is reflexive – it incorporates discourses. As agriculture has become more scientific, more industrialised, its reflexivity has been enhanced – the action (both linguistic and non-linguistic) has become more reflexive, more thoroughly shaped by discourses. The point is that social practices vary and change in their degree of reflexivity, and therefore in how important discourses are to the action. So, summing up, language (as genre) remains a relatively secondary part of the action (agricultural work), but increasingly important in the discourses which ever more thoroughly shape the action.

On the other hand, language is a very important part of the action in the social practice of government – much of the action of government *is* language. But there is also a special relationship between action and discourses in (democratic) government. It is an inherent property of the practice of democratic government that action arises from public contestation between discourses – discourses are deployed by different parties and groups to win sufficient political support for particular visions of the world to act.

I suggested in the Introduction that this inherent importance of language in government is enhanced in the case of New Labour. New Labour's promotional way of governing means that language becomes an even more important part of the action of government, for instance as part of the management of perception through 'media spin'. I have suggested that this centralising tendency in New Labour's way of governing is in tension with a move to decentralise and disperse government, a move towards a more 'network' style of government. In so far as this becomes a reality, it also entails language becoming a more important part of the action – that is what the current interest in 'deliberative democracy' means: that the effectiveness of forms of deliberation and dialogue becomes crucial to the effectiveness of government. Also, the move to 'cultural governance' (see chapter 2), government through the management of culture, implies an increased importance for discourses in shaping the action – managing culture means gaining acceptance for particular representations of the social world, i.e. particular discourses. And, finally, if it is true as I suggested in the Introduction that New Labour seeks to reconcile in language what cannot be reconciled in reality given their commitment to neo-liberalism – neo-liberal 'enterprise' and 'social justice' – that also enhances the importance of political discourse.

I referred above to the dangers of the 'turn to discourse' – seeing social life as nothing but discourse. This sort of extreme 'discourse theory' makes it impossible to recognise the distinctions I have just been making. If everything is discourse, there is of course no way of differentiating social practices in terms of the relative importance of discourse, or tracing changes over time within a particular social practice. Yet it is crucial to be able to do so – we cannot take the importance of language for granted, we need to establish it case by case.

Many political theorists and analysts recognise the importance of language in politics and government, especially in contemporary societies.[11] But there is an important difference between much of this work and the approach I have adopted. It is one thing to recognise that language is important, it is another thing to see the detailed analysis of texts as important, which is my position. I referred for instance to Ruth Levitas' analysis of the discourses of 'social exclusion' in chapter 2. I think it is a very good analysis, but it is not what I would regard as text analysis. Why is it important to look at the detail of texts? What does my style of analysis add to Levitas', or to those of the other analysts referred to in note 11 of this chapter?

Let me answer this question by referring readers back to chapter 3, and particularly the analysis of the long extract in the section entitled 'Change in the political discourse of New Labour'. What I was arguing there was that texts are processes in which political work is done – work on elaborating political discourses, as well as the rhetorical work of mobilising people behind political discourses. I analysed the elaboration of the political discourse in that example as the weaving together of different discourses through relations of equivalence, antithesis, and entailment. I was focusing on what we might call the 'texture' of the text, its distinctive form of materiality. And that is what text analysis adds to the sort of discourse analysis that Levitas does: it shows how the work of politics or government is partly done in the material of texts – it gets into the texture of texts, so the political and governmental processes which are going on there can be unpicked. Without text analysis, we simply miss this important aspect of political and governmental work.

The approach I have adopted to analysing discourse in the book is known as 'critical discourse analysis'.[12] Critical discourse analysis sees language as one element of a social practice along the lines of what I said at the beginning of this chapter. The aim is to see how language is articulated together with other elements. This approach is particularly concerned with social change as it affects discourse, and with how it connects with social relations of power and domination. It looks at change in terms of how the combination of discourses, genres, and styles, which make up the language elements of a social practice, changes over time. In the case of New Labour, the political discourse of the 'Third Way' has brought new right and social democratic discourses, as well as communitarian discourses into a new combination; changes in the way of governing have taken the form of changes in the set of genres which are brought together in government; and Blair's rhetorical style is a distinctive combination of public and private styles. Critical discourse analysis aims to trace these changes through close analysis of the texture of texts, for reasons I have just discussed.

Is there an alternative?

New Labour is operating in a field it did not create and which it might well not have chosen. A purely negative critique, which ignores the difficult circumstances, is itself open to question. Are there realistic alternatives? I think there are. It is important to distinguish between an electoral campaign and being in government with a large majority – in the former there is little people can do to change the field, in the latter there may be quite a lot.

I want to conclude therefore with three broad recommendations. These are ways in which New Labour could leave politics and government better than they found it. They are about language, but since language always goes with other things they are not just about language. I am not suggesting that dramatic changes can be achieved in any of them within four or even eight years, but worthwhile changes are within reach.

1. Dialogue. Perhaps the most fundamental contribution New Labour could make is in taking measures to encourage and facilitate real dialogue and debate in the sense I suggested earlier and repeat here. In real dialogue:

   - People decide to come together, and can come back together.
   - Access is open for whichever section of society wants to join in – there is 'equality of opportunity' to join and to contribute.
   - People are free to disagree, and the differences are recognised.

- There is space for consensus to be reached, alliances to be formed – but no guarantees.
- It is talk that makes a difference – it leads to action (e.g. policy change).

2. Difference. New Labour's political discourse could be made more open to difference – by avoiding a language of consensus (e.g. a vague and bland 'one-nation' *we*) which disguises differences, by avoiding polar divisions which misrepresent people as divided neatly into two (e.g. 'old left' and 'new right'), by acknowledging differences within the Government.
3. Honesty. New Labour could shift away from designing its language quite so much on the basis of market research and focus groups, away from its preoccupation with 'spin' and with how to say things in ways that will win support, away from designing its leadership styles on the basis of calculations of effects. Long-term trust cannot be built on this basis. On the contrary, it results in contempt for politics. The Government can contribute to the long trek towards political health by recognising that trust is a two-way relation – by beginning to trust people with the truth as its members see it, warts and all.

The Government will not, I imagine, be that eager to take up these recommendations. Nevertheless, we must keep emphasising this: the way things are does not exhaust the possibilities for the way things could be.

GLOSSARY

The first occurrence of each of these terms is highlighted with an asterisk in the main text.

antithesis Texts simultaneously create differences and reduce differences – they set up antitheses and equivalences★ between words and phrases. Antitheses set up a contrast, often marked by a move from positive to negative or vice versa, 'x not y', as in 'the stakeholder economy involves all our people, not a privileged few'. Other markers of antithesis include 'but' and 'rather than'.

collocation Collocations are co-occurrences between words in a text. For instance, we might look at the collocations of the word 'values' to see which adjectives most frequently modify it in the language of New Labour (adjectives like 'shared' and 'traditional' are quite common, as is 'British', but 'socialist values' does not occur – see pp. 47–8). Or we might look at 'social exclusion' to see which verbs it occurs as the object of – does government 'prevent' social exclusion, or rather 'reduce' it? See pp. 55–6.

equivalences Texts simultaneously create differences and reduce differences – they set up antitheses★ and equivalences between words and phrases. Equivalences are often set up through lists.★ For example, the items listed in the second sentence are set up as equivalences: 'We all know this is a world of dramatic change. In technology; in trade; in media and communications; in the new global economy refashioning our industries and capital markets.' Equivalences can also be set up by substitutions. For instance, 'British business' is substituted for 'we' as the subject of 'compete' in the following example, and so they are set up as equivalent: 'In the increasingly global economy of today we cannot compete in the old way. British business must compete by …'.

lists Lists are very simple and obvious features of texts, but they can

161

be quite important. A list is a series of two or more items conjoined together (with or without a conjunction – generally *and* – marking their connection). In traditional grammatical terms, lists are 'paratactic' (their elements are equal, one is not subordinate to another). Items in lists are equivalences.* Where lists are heavily used as in the language of New Labour, they may indicate what I called in chapter 1 (discussing 'the cascade of change') a logic of appearances – things are connected only in so far as they appear together, and no deeper explanations are sought.

metaphor The concept of metaphor will be familiar to most readers. Although metaphors are most often talked about in literary texts, they are an important part of all sorts of language use, including political and governmental language. It is usually possible to metaphorise something in various ways, and the choice of metaphor can be socially significant. For instance, it is animals and people who 'migrate', so if technology is represented as 'migrating', it is treated as having animal or human qualities – as if it moved around on the basis of its own instincts or decisions. This metaphor backgrounds the activities and responsibilities of the people who make technology move.

modality The modality of a particular sentence is the speaker's or writer's level of commitment to the claim it makes or the obligation it expresses. There are two main aspects of modality – one is to do with truth, the other with obligation. In terms of truth-modality, commitment to the truth of a claim can be categorical (e.g. 'there's no future in that for Britain') or modulated to various degrees (e.g. 'I don't think there's any future in that for Britain'). Categorical modality sounds authoritative. In terms of obligation-modality, the same distinction applies: compare the categorical 'it is essential not to end up walking away' (or 'you mustn't end up walking away') with 'you shouldn't end up walking away'.

mood The grammatical moods of English are: declarative, interrogative, imperative. Every sentence is in one of these moods. Systematic preferences can be socially or ideologically significant. For instance, the Green Paper on welfare reform (discussed in chapter 5) consists overwhelmingly of declarative sentences. Even though it is a consultation document, there are few interrogative sentences: there is more telling going on than asking.

nominalisation Nominalisation is the representation of a process* as a noun – for instance the process of various aspects of social life changing in particular ways as simply 'change' (e.g. 'change sweeps the world'). Nominalisation characteristically means vagueness – no specification of what is changing, in what ways, over what period of time, and so forth. One possible consequence links nominalisation to passive★ – agency and responsibility can be obfuscated.

over-wording Over-wording is the proliferation of different words in the same area of meaning, for instance the words associated with partnership in the language of New Labour – 'partnership', 'cooperation', 'consultation', 'dialogue', 'working (bringing, coming) together', and so forth. Over-wording may be indicative of 'intense ideological preoccupation'[1] – suggesting that a particular area of meaning is especially significant or problematic.

passive English sentences with transitive action processes★ are either 'active' (e.g. 'the multinationals can make goods in low-cost countries') or 'passive' (e.g. 'goods can be made in low-cost countries [by the multinationals]'). Passives can occur with or without agents (phrases with the preposition 'by'). Agents can be omitted for various reasons – perhaps because they are obvious, but also perhaps as a way of obfuscating agency and responsibility.

presupposition Texts are always a mixture of explicit and implicit meaning – what is said and what is presupposed, taken as given. Sometimes what is presupposed is uncontentious – simply common-sense knowledge. But many presuppositions are contentious – they take for granted things which are questionable. For instance, 'no country is immune from the massive change that globalisation brings' presupposes that 'globalisation' is a simple matter of fact. Presuppositions are marked in various ways in texts – a definite article ('the') is the most common marker (e.g. 'This is simply a recognition of the challenge the modern world poses.' presupposes that the modern world poses a challenge – and that 'the modern world' exists).

processes The English language distinguishes several types of process: actions, either transitive (with two participants, an agent, and an 'affected' – or, in tradition terms, the 'object') or intransitive (with one participant); relations – of 'being' (what I call 'attribution') or 'having'; mental processes – such as thinking, seeing, liking; and verbal process – saying, claiming, etc. There is often a socially or ideologically significant choice between different process types – as in the case discussed on p. 24.

pronouns   'We' is a New Labour 'keyword' (see the Introduction). There is a standard distinction between 'exclusive' and 'inclusive' uses of 'we' – the former excludes those addressed, the latter includes them. So sometimes 'we' means just the Government (or the Party), and sometimes it means something like 'the people of Britain'. A problem with 'inclusive we' is knowing how universal or particular it is, and who exactly it includes.

'It' is often vague (see examples in chapter 1). The pronoun 'I' is quite common in some contexts – Blair sometimes oscillates between a collective 'we' and an individual 'I' in his speeches. He also sometimes uses 'you' in a non-specific way (e.g. 'you've got to go over their heads to a large extent', which is equivalent to 'one has to ...', but belongs to everyday language – Blair the 'normal person'). See chapter 4.

NOTES

PREFACE: BIN THE SPIN!

1 Gould 1998: 219
2 Hall 1998

INTRODUCTION

1 Prescott 1998
2 Prescott 1999
3 Barnett 1998, Blair 1998a, Clark and Newman 1997, Osborne and Gaebler 1993, Perri 6 1997, 1998
4 Blair 1998a
5 Franklin 1998: 4
6 Blair 1998a
7 Platt 1998
8 Blair 1997a
9 See Montgomery 1999 for a fuller analysis of this speech. Montgomery discusses how Blair's hesitancy and pausing in delivery may have contributed to the impression that he was sincere.
10 Gould 1998
11 Rentoul 1997
12 Blair 1998c
13 Blair 1998d
14 Hall 1998, Marquand 1998
15 Ranciere 1995, Dillon 1998
16 Barnett 1998, Hall 1998 – though see Mulgan 1998 for a different view
17 Department of Social Security 1998a
18 I am grateful to Costas Iordanidis for the formulation in this paragraph.
19 The New Labour corpus consists of fifty-three speeches by Tony Blair given between 1997–9, as well as one speech by Gordon Brown; five interviews with Blair; four written documents including the 1997 'Labour Manifesto' and 'Summary' chapters from the Green Papers on welfare reform and pension reform, as well as the White Paper on competition. The smaller corpus of earlier Labour material mainly covers the period 1973–82, though there is one speech from 1964 and the 1987 manifesto. The corpus includes three speeches by former Labour

leaders, the 1974, 1979, and 1987 manifestos, and eight other written texts. The two corpora differ in various ways, notably in that the New Labour corpus is mainly speeches, whereas the earlier one is mainly written. Comparisons based on these corpora give only rough indications of what is distinctive about New Labour.

20 I have arrived at this list of keywords by comparing three much fuller lists. Two are based upon comparisons between the New Labour corpus and much larger corpora – the British National Corpus of Written Texts and a corpus of texts from the *Guardian* newspaper. The third is based on comparison between the New Labour and earlier Labour corpora. I have included in my list words that are common to the top sixty keywords in all three corpora.

21 Hall 1998

1 THE 'THIRD WAY': THE POLITICAL DISCOURSE OF NEW LABOUR

1 Department of Trade and Industry 1998
2 Blair 1998c
3 Blair 1999a
4 Bourdieu 1998
5 Held 1998
6 Clarke and Newman 1998
7 Blair 1998e
8 Blair 1998a
9 Blair 1999a
10 Blair 1999a
11 Blair 1999b
12 Rentoul 1997: 485ff.
13 Keat and Abercrombie 1991
14 Blair 1999a, Department of Trade and Industry 1998
15 Fairclough 1991
16 Quotations are from Blair 1998c
17 Brown 1994
18 Examples are from Blair 1998c
19 Blair 1998c
20 Blair 1998c
21 Blair 1998c
22 Blair 1998c
23 Driver and Martell 1998, Gould 1998, Rentoul 1997. According to Levitas 1998, the version of communitarianism Blair has been influenced by is closer to Amitai Etzioni's.
24 Rentoul 1997
25 Blair 1999a
26 Brown 1998
27 Gould 1998
28 Rentoul 1997: 279–80
29 Blair 1999c
30 Blair 1994a
31 Blair 1998d, 1998c

32 Blair 1998a
33 Blair 1998a
34 Blair 1999d, 1999a
35 Blair 1999a
36 Blair 1999b
37 For a more detailed discussion see Driver and Martell 1998: 26–31
38 Gould 1998
39 Blair 1994b
40 Bourdieu 1991
41 Blair 1995
42 Livingstone 1998
43 Blair 1999a
44 Blunkett 1998
45 Piper 1998

2 THE LANGUAGE OF 'SOCIAL EXCLUSION'

1 Mandelson 1997
2 Blair 1997b
3 Room 1995
4 Blair 1997c
5 Mandelson 1997
6 Blair 1997b
7 Social Exclusion Unit 1997
8 Levitas 1998
9 Blair1997d
10 Mandelson 1997
11 Harman 1997
12 Mandelson 1997
13 Townsend 1997
14 Berghman 1995
15 SEU 1997
16 European Foundation for the Improvement of Living and Working Conditions, 1995
17 See Levitas 1998
18 Harman 1997
19 Marquand 1998
20 Demos 1997: 3–4
21 MacDonald 1994: 525
22 Jordan 1996
23 Blair 1999b
24 Blair 1997d
25 Levitas 1998

3 THE MAKING OF THE LANGUAGE OF NEW LABOUR

1 Jessop 1998
2 Gould 1998
3 Rentoul 1997: 285–7

NOTES

4 Driver and Martell 1998
5 Blair 1998a
6 Clinton 1996: 43–4
7 Swinton Lecture, July 1979, in Thatcher 1989: 89
8 Blair 1998c
9 Blair 1999c
10 Piper 1998
11 European Commission 1998
12 'European Foundation for the Improvement of Living and Working Conditions' 1994
13 Blair 1999e
14 Wacquant 1999
15 Wacquant 1999: 1
16 Bourdieu and Wacquant 1998
17 World Bank 1994
18 World Bank 1999
19 Barratt Brown and Coates 1996: 172–4
20 Barratt Brown and Coates 1996: 177–8
21 'Counter Information' 1998, 50
22 Commission on Social Justice 1994
23 Levitas 1998, chapter 2
24 Phillips 1993, 1998
25 Gould 1998: 255
26 Aristotle's account of political rhetoric in the *Rhetoric* (1991) captures this duality
27 Blair 1996a
28 Blair 1996b
29 Gould 1998
30 Blair 1996a
31 Driver and Martell 1998
32 Blair 1996e
33 Blair 1999a

4 THE RHETORICAL STYLE OF TONY BLAIR

1 Gould 1998: 211
2 Blair 1997b, 1999f
3 Rentoul 1997: 432–3
4 Blair 1997a
5 Gould 1998: 211
6 'The Swinton lecture', July 1979, Thatcher 1989: 94
7 Blair 1999b
8 Hall 1998

5 THE LANGUAGE OF GOVERNMENT

1 Blair 1996f
2 Driver and Martell 1998, Hall 1998, Marquand 1998
3 Clarke and Newman 1997
4 Barnett 1998

5   Marquand 1988, Hutton 1995, Driver and Martell 1998
6   Barnett 1998
7   Blair 1998d
8   Jones 1999
9   Jones 1999
10   Department of Social Security 1998
11   Perri 6 1995, 1997, 1998
12   Perri 6 1998
13   Blair 1996d
14   Blair 1998a
15   Blair 1996d
16   Arendt 1958, Fairclough 1999, Habermas 1989, Held 1998, Touraine
     1996
17   The Labour Party 1997
18   Department of Social Security 1998b
19   Department of Social Security 1998a
20   Jones 1999
21   Department of Social Security 1999
22   Blair 1999c
23   See Giddens 1998
24   Fowler, *et al.* 1979

6 RHETORIC AND REALITY: KOSOVO

1   Taylor 1999
2   See Dant 1991, Billig 1996, Potter and Wetherell 1987, Laclau and
     Mouffe 1985
3   Chouliaraki and Fairclough 1999, Harvey 1996
4   Harvey 1996
5   See Chouliaraki and Fairclough 1999 for a discussion of the complex
     issues involved.
6   Note that the term 'discourse' is commonly used in different ways. It is
     used in an abstract sense for the language element of social practices – I
     have just used 'language' to avoid the ambiguity. And it is used in the
     more concrete sense of this paragraph. In the abstract sense, it is used
     without an article ('a', 'the'), and only in the singular – e.g. 'discourse is
     one element of social practices'; in the more concrete sense it is used
     with an article ('a' or 'the') and can be made plural – e.g. 'the discourse
     of New Labour, and other political discourses'.
7   Blair 1996e
8   Blair 1999b
9   Billig 1999
10   New Left Review 1999
11   See for instance Laclau and Mouffe 1985, Levitas 1998, Hall and Jacques
     1983
12   See Fairclough 1989, 1992, 1995, and Fairclough and Chouliaraki 1999

GLOSSARY

1   Fowler *et al.* 1979

SOURCES

Tony Blair (1994a) Speech to the Family Breakdown and Criminal Activity Conference, 24 May

Tony Blair (1994b) Speech at the National Film Theatre

Tony Blair (1995) *Time* magazine, 30 November

Tony Blair (1996a) Speech to Singapore Business Community, 8 January

Tony Blair (1996b) Speech in the Assembly Rooms, Derby, 18 January

Tony Blair (1996c) 'Faith in the City – Ten Years On', Southwark Cathedral, 29 January

Tony Blair (1996d) John Smith Memorial lecture, 7 February

Tony Blair (1996e) Speech at the Freedom of Information awards, 25 March

Tony Blair (1996f) Article in *The Economist*, September

Tony Blair (1997a) Statement on the death of Princess Diana, August

Tony Blair (1997b) Speech to the Labour Party Annual Conference, September

Tony Blair (1997c) Speech at the Aylesbury estate, 2 June

Tony Blair (1997d) Speech for the Social Exclusion Unit launch, 8 December

Tony Blair (1998a) 'The Third Way: New Politics for the New Century', Fabian Society pamphlet

Tony Blair (1998b) Interview with Sir David Frost, 29 April

Tony Blair (1998c) Speech at the Confederation of British Industry Annual Dinner 27 May

Tony Blair (1998d) 'Publication of Annual Report', 30 July

Tony Blair (1998e) 'The Patriotic Case for Internationalism', Hong Kong 9 October

Tony Blair (1999a) 'Facing the Modern Challenge: the Third Way in Britain and South Africa', 6 January

Tony Blair (1999b) 'Doctrine of the International Community', Chicago, 22 April

Tony Blair (1999c) 'It really is the end of the something for nothing days', *Daily Mail*, 10 February

Tony Blair (1999d)Speech to the IPPR, 14 January

Tony Blair (1999e) 'Beveridge lecture', 16 March

Tony Blair (1999f) 'Breakfast with Frost', BBC1, 10 January

David Blunkett (1998) 'Foreword' to Department of Education and Employment 1998

Gordon Brown (1994) 'Fair is Efficient', Fabian Society pamphlet

Gordon Brown (1998) Parliamentary speech on the Government's spending review, July

Michael Barratt Brown and Ken Coates (1996) *The Blair Revelation*, Nottingham: Spokesman Books

Bill Clinton (1996) *Between Hope and History: Meeting America's Challenges for the 21st Century*, New York: Random House

'A dud deal' (1998) in *Counter Information*, no. 50

Alistair Darling (1999) Press release ('Fight against poverty'), 18 February

Harriet Harman (1997) Speech at the launching of the Centre for Analysis of Social Exclusion, London School of Economics, 13 November

Ken Livingstone (1998) Review of A. Giddens 'The Third Way', *The New Statesman*, 25 September

Peter Mandelson (1997) 'Labour's next steps: tackling social exclusion', 14 August

Peter Mandelson (1998) Press Statement, publication of the Department of Trade and Industry, 16 December 1998

John Prescott (1998) Interview reported in the *Independent*, 30 December 1998

John Prescott (1999) Interview on BBC Radio 4 'Today' programme, 4 January

Margaret Thatcher (1989) *The Revival of Britain: Speeches on Home and European Affairs*, London: Aurum Press

Department of Education and Employment (1998) 'The Learning Age' (Green Paper) London: The Stationery Office

Department of Social Security (1998a) 'New Ambitions for Our Country: A New Contract for Welfare' (Green Paper on Welfare Reform), London: The Stationery Office

Department of Social Security (1998b) 'A New Contract for Welfare: Partnership in Pensions' (Green Paper), London: The Stationery Office

Department of Trade and Industry (1998) 'Building the Knowledge-Driven Economy' (White Paper), London: The Stationery Office

European Commission (1998) 'Teaching and Learning: Towards the Learning Society' (White Paper on Education)

European Foundation for the Improvement of Living and Working Conditions (1994) 'Bridging the Gulf: Improving Social Cohesion in Europe', Shankill, Ireland

European Foundation for the Improvement of Living and Working Conditions (1995) 'For Citizens and against Exclusion: the Role of Public Welfare Services' Shankill, Ireland

Labour Party (1997) 'Labour into Power: a Framework for Partnership' London: Labour Party

Social Exclusion Unit (1997) 'The Social Exclusion Unit' (leaflet) London: The Cabinet Office

World Bank (1994) 'Averting the Old Age Crisis: Policies to Protect the Old and Promote Growth'

World Bank (1999) 'A Proposal for a Comprehensive Development Framework'

REFERENCES

Arendt, H. (1958) *The Human Condition*, Chicago: Chicago University Press

Aristotle (1991) *The Art of Rhetoric*, trans. by H. C. Lawson-Tancred, London: Penguin

Barnett, A. (1998) 'All power to the citizens', *Marxism Today*, special edition on New Labour, 44–7

Berghman, J. (1995) 'Social exclusion in Europe: policy context and analytical framework', in G. Room (ed.) (1995) *Beyond the Threshold: the Measurement and Analysis of Social Exclusion*, Bristol: The Policy Press

Billig, M. (1996) *Arguing and Thinking*, new edn, Cambridge: Cambridge University Press

Billig, M. (1999) 'Commodity, fetishism and repression: reflections on Marx and Freud and the psychology of consumer capitalism' to appear in *Theory and Psychology*

Bourdieu, P. (1991) *Language and Symbolic Power*, Cambridge: Polity Press

Bourdieu, P. (1998) 'A reasoned utopia and economic fatalism', *New Left Review*, 227: 25–30

Bourdieu, P. and Wacquant, L. (1998) '*Les ruses de la raison imperialiste*', *Actes de la recherche en sciences sociales*, Vol. 121–2

Calhoun, C. (1995) *Critical Social Theory*, Oxford: Blackwell

Chouliaraki, L. and Fairclough, N. (1999) *Discourse in Late Modernity: Rethinking Critical Discourse Analysis*, Edinburgh: Edinburgh University Press

Clarke, J. and Newman, J. (1997) *The Managerial State*, London: Sage

Clarke, J. and Newman, J. (1998) 'A modern British people? New Labour and the reconstruction of social welfare', Occasional Paper, Department of Intercultural Communication and Management, Copenhagen Business School

Dant, T. (1991) *Knowledge, Ideology and Discourse*, London: Routledge

Demos (1997) 'The wealth and poverty of nations: tackling social exclusion' *Demos Quarterly*, Issue 12

Dillon, M. (1998) 'The objectification of politics', Working Paper, Politics Department, Lancaster University

Driver, S. and Martell, L. (1998) *New Labour: Politics after Thatcherism*, Cambridge: Polity Press

Fairclough, N. (1989) *Language and Power* London: Longmans

Fairclough, N. (1991) 'What might we mean by "enterprise discourse"?', in R. Keat and N. Abercrombie, *Enterprise Culture*, London: Routledge, pp. 38–57

Fairclough, N. (1992) *Discourse and Social Change*, Cambridge: Polity Press

Fairclough, N. (1995) *Critical Discourse Analysis*, London: Longmans

Fairclough, N. (1999) 'Democracy and the public sphere in critical research on discourse', in R. Wodak and C. Ludwig (eds) *Challenges in a Changing World: Issues in Critical Discourse Analysis*, Vienna: Passagen Verlag

Fairclough, N. (2000) 'Discourse, social theory, and social research: the discourse of welfare reform', *Journal of Sociolinguistics*, Vol. 4

Fowler, R., Hodge, R., Kress, G. and Trew, T. (eds) (1979) *Language and Control*, London: Routledge

Franklin, B. (1998) *Tough on Soundbites, Tough on the Causes of Soundbites: New Labour and News Management*, Catalyst Paper 3, London: Catalyst Trust

Giddens, A. (1998) *The Third Way: the Renewal of Social Democracy*, Cambridge: Polity Press

Gould, P. (1998) *The Unfinished Revolution: How the Modernisers Saved the Labour Party*, London: Little, Brown & Co

Habermas, J. (1971) *Knowledge and Human Interests*, Boston: Beacon Press

Habermas, J. (1989) *The Structural Transformation of the Public Sphere*, Cambridge: Polity Press

Hall, S. (1998) 'The great moving nowhere show', *Marxism Today*, special issue on New Labour, pp. 9–14

Harvey, D. (1996) *Justice, Nature and the Geography of Difference*, Oxford: Blackwell

Held, D. (1998) 'Globalisation: the timid tendency', *Marxism Today*, special issue on New Labour, pp. 24–7

Hutton, W. (1995) *The State We're In*, London: Jonathan Cape

Jessop, B. (1998) 'Reflections on globalisation and its (Il)logic(s)', Working Paper, Sociology Department, Lancaster University

Jones, N. (1999) *Sultans of Spin: the Media and the New Labour Government*, London: Victor Gollancz

Jordan, B. (1996) *A Theory of Poverty and Social Exclusion*, Cambridge: Polity Press

Keat, R. and Abercrombie, N. (1991) *Enterprise Culture*, London: Routledge

Laclau, E. and Mouffe, C. (1985) *Hegemony and Socialist Strategy*, London: Verso

Levitas, R. (1998) *The Inclusive Society? Social Exclusion and New Labour*, London: Macmillan

MacDonald, R. (1994) 'Fiddly jobs, undeclared working and the something for nothing society', *Work Employment and Society*, 8.4: 507–30

Marquand, D. (1988) *The Unprincipled Society: new Demands and Old Politics*, London: Fontana

Marquand, D. (1998) 'The Blair paradox', *Prospect*, 19–22 May

Montgomery, M. (1999) 'Speaking sincerely: public reactions to the death of Diana', *Language and Literature*, 7: 5–33

Mulgan, G. (1998) 'Whinge and a prayer', *Marxism Today*, special issue on New Labour, pp. 15–16

New Left Review, 234 March/April 1999, 'The Imperialism of Human Rights'

Osborne, D. and Gaebler, T. (1993) *Reinventing Government*, New York: Plume Books

Perri 6 (1995) 'Governing by cultures', *Demos Quarterly*, Issue 7, London: Demos

Perri 6 (1997) *Holistic Government*, London: Demos

Perri 6 (1998) 'Problem-solving government', in I. Hargreaves and I. Christie (eds) *Tomorrow's Politics*, London: Demos

Phillips, L. (1993) 'Discourse and Themesong Rhetoric: Reproduction and Transformation of the Discourse of Thatcherism across Socio-Political Domains', Ph.D thesis, London School of Economics

Phillips, L. (1998) 'Hegemony and political discourse: the lasting impact of Thatcherism', *Sociology*, 32: 847–67

Piper, A. (1998) 'Lifelong learning, human capital and the soundbite', draft paper

Platt, S. (1998) 'Government by Task Force', Catalyst Paper 2, London: Catalyst

Potter, J. and Wetherell, M. (1987) *Discourse and Social Psychology*, London: Sage

Ranciere, J. (1995) *On the Shores of Politics*, London: Verso

Rentoul, J. (1997) *Tony Blair*, revised edn, London: Warner Books

Room, G. (ed.) (1995) *Beyond the Threshold: the Measurement and Analysis of Social Exclusion*, Bristol: The Policy Press

Taylor, M. (1999) 'Takes sides but open the debate', *Red Pepper*, June

Touraine, A. (1996) *What is Democracy?*, Boulder, Col.: Westview Press

Townsend, P. (1997) 'Redistribution: the strategic alternative to privatisation', in A. Walker and C. Walker (eds) *Britain Divided: the Growth of Social Exclusion in the 1980s and 1990s*, London: Child Poverty Action Group

Wacquant, L. (1999) 'Ce vent punitif qui vient d'Amérique', *Le Monde Diplomatique*, April

INDEX